LIFE IS A TREASURE HUNT

By Joseph R. Fraia with Deborah Sanguineti

Published by

Sinkrom Corporation

Publisher's Note

This publication is designed to provide accurate and authoritative information in regard to the subject matter covered. It is sold with the understanding that the publisher is not engaged in rendering psychological, financial, legal, or other professional services. If expert assistance or counseling is needed, the services of a competent professional should be sought.

Email: info@lifeisatreasurehunt.com

Website: www.lifeisatreasurehunt.com

Instagram: @lifeisatreasurehunt

Facebook: @lifeisatreasurehunt

Joseph Ralph Fraia and Deborah Sanguineti

Authors / Editorial Directors

The *Integrative Identity Development System* and the *Seven Tools for the Treasure Hunt* are trademarks of Joseph Ralph Fraia and Deborah Sanguineti

Copyright © 2021 by Joseph Ralph Fraia and Deborah Sanguineti

Joseph Ralph Fraia and Deborah Sanguineti assert their moral right to be identified as the authors of this work.

Cover by Julia Roach

Illustrations by Ron Roach

All rights reserved. No part of this publication may be reproduced, distributed, or transmitted in any form or by any means, electronic or mechanical, including photocopying, recording, or any information storage and retrieval system, without permission in writing from both authors Joseph Ralph Fraia and Deborah Sanguineti.

ISBN-13: 978-0-578-95810-1

Printed in the United States of America

My gratitude and my love go to
My wife Xiaoting, for loving me for the man I am.
My family, for making me the man I am.
Deborah, for helping me becoming the man I want to be.

Thank you to Joseph
for entrusting me with his vision and igniting my spirit of adventure.
Thank you to my nearest and dearest family and friends who supported me and encouraged me every step of the way. I needed you more than I let on.
I couldn't have asked for better teams.

'None are more hopelessly enslaved than those who falsely believe they are free'

- Johann Wolfgang von Goethe

'Per aspera ad Astra'

- Lucius Annaeus Seneca

CONTENTS

Introduction..6

PART I
Introspection
Integrative Identity Development System™

Chapter 1 - Your Consciousness is your Superpower................24

Chapter 2 - The Ladder of Inference: the traditional approach......28

Chapter 3 - Enhanced Ladder of Inference............................37

Chapter 4 - Break the bars of your invisible cage.....................45

PART II
Spirit of Adventure
The Seven Tools for the Treasure Hunt™

Chapter 1 - Discovery...55

Chapter 2 - Mission...65

Chapter 3 - Map...73

Chapter 4 - Compass..83

Chapter 5 - Team..94

Chapter 6 - Vehicle..110

Chapter 7 - Treasure...122

Afterword.. 139

References...141

About the Authors..142

'Break the bars of your invisible cage. Master your fears, embrace change, achieve Higher Consciousness.
Your Treasure awaits.'

Introduction

by Joseph R. Fraia

The scientific premise: Integrative Therapy

This book follows the teachings and the results of the latest developments in the Integrative Therapy approach, based on the utilization of the most effective tools in Western Psychology and Eastern Medicine, to mold a combined approach to psychotherapy that brings together different elements of specific therapies.

I firmly and passionately believe in the idea that there are many ways in which human psychology can be explored and understood, and no 'one theory' alone holds all the answers.

It is a revolutionary approach because it uses techniques and methods separately tested and used for centuries, and even millennia, in their respective cultures, but only recently combined together to forge a new omni-comprehensive discipline aimed at the betterment of the Self and of Society.

The integrative approach also refers to the infusion of a person's personality and needs, integrating the affective, behavioral, cognitive, and physiological systems within one person, and addressing social and spiritual complexions. Essentially, as an intuitive coach and integrative counselor, I am not only concerned with what works but why it works, tailoring my counseling to a person and not the person to the counseling.

In line with the latest and most advanced findings and techniques in integrative therapy, I have created my feature methods 'Integrative Identity Development System™ and Seven Tools for the Treasure Hunt™,' and furthered their concepts and development with my co-author Deborah Sanguineti.

The results of this method are embodied in this book to provide you - the reader - with a simple and practical step-by-step guide that will be the toolbox that will lead you throughout the hunt to your own Treasure.

Once you have read this book, you will realize why so many people over the years, including Deborah and myself, have greatly benefited from the transformational experience of defeating your fears and embracing change.

The reasons our methods work is because they teach you the following:
- To look at life as a treasure hunt.
- Looking at life as a quest tingles our innate spirit of adventure.
- The art of letting go, not holding on to grief, and not taking yourself too seriously.
- The commitment to build yourself as an expert in recognizing the challenges in your life, what you need to overcome those challenges, how to achieve your goals, and how to move beyond your goals.

- A clear purpose in life: find your Treasure.
- The relief and satisfaction of knowing there is a reward at the conclusion of this journey we call Life.

Let's start this journey together.

Stirring the pot

What happens when you pinch the chords of your subconscious? When you stir the pot of your daily routine and open your mind to the possibility of doing something different from the ordinary, that would make YOU feel better?

That is the universal and timeless fascination we, as humans, have for the ideal of 'the journey.'

As soon as we picture ourselves going from a point A to a point B, we start rationalizing that event as an experience, an adventure: before we embark ourselves on it, we want to understand where the destination is, how we will find it, if other people are going to be with us, how we are going to get there and what we are going to find at the point of our destination.

But above everything, we want to know why. Why should we leave the comfort and security of the 'here and now' to explore an unknown 'there and later'?

The answers to these very fundamental and existential questions are what we will provide in this book, and, spoiler alert, you got the most significant clue in the title.

Life is a treasure hunt. It is, indeed. Not inherently or necessarily, though, and that is why you become the crucial part of the equation of your existence.

Life simply happens. Some things you can control, many others, most of them actually, you can't. Broader religious or philosophical beliefs are separated or independent from the fact we just stated.

Believing in God, a prophet, a philosophy, a great architect, science, spirits, or nature, does not change the practical material truth that some things you can control, but most of them you can't: per se, this is a condition we cannot change, so brooding about it won't really help us.

Once someone realizes this fundamental condition of our existence, something interesting can happen.

Instead of focusing on 'why' it is that there are things we can or can't control, we can start instead to pay more attention to 'how' we can give meaning and purpose to our existence.

How can we work on the things we can control so that the things we can't control will have a lesser impact on our lives?

How can we achieve this goal? How can we conduct a meaningful and purposeful existence?

Good questions. To answer them, let's continue to the next paragraph.

Humankind is united by its one purpose: to find the meaning of Life.

One of the fascinating aspects of humankind is that we wonder what our origin is, what are the meaning and the purpose of our lives.

We are the only living creatures (that we know of) who have developed consciousness and awareness of our Self and our existence as both an individual and in relation to the people and environment around us.

As far as we can go back to recorded history, we have proof and records that humans have always perceived that life is simply more than just waking up in the morning – eating – mating – reproducing – surviving – going to sleep and dying.

In search of what is this 'more' that gives a sense to our existence, we have conceived and elaborated gods, idols, philosophies, religions, ideologies, cultures, and all the isms you can think of. And yet, we are still looking for what is that 'something' capable of explaining to us 'why' and 'what for' we exist.

It is very comforting and inspiring to realize that humankind, despite the inherent differences of race and habitat and therefore cultures, is unified by an essential common denominator: give meaning to our existence.

In this book, Higher Consciousness is the underlying theme and the ultimate tool to answer the ultimate question: what is the purpose of life?

What is the answer? The Treasure: to live a meaningful life.

'How do I live a meaningful life,' you might wonder? This book will give you the tools to do that.

Integrative Therapy and Higher Consciousness

From Eastern medicine and traditions, we have learned how beneficial can be, and to some extent necessary, to meditate and to embrace a holistic/spiritual approach in life, if we want to improve our wellbeing.

From Western psychotherapy and psychiatry, we have learned what a determinant importance biological factors can have and the relevance of traumatic experiences in defining our behaviors; concepts that can be helpful and highly beneficial for some people to deal with their issues and resolve them.

But none of the above are enough. They are incomplete. They both miss something.

Eastern medicine and traditions alone do not take into consideration enough the determinism of genetic features and chemical imbalances as well as social constructs and systemic structures of contemporary societies. They are generally based on pure intuitive reasoning, i.e., theories according to which knowledge is achieved not through analytical reasoning but rather through perception, emotional intelligence and empathic connection to nature and other human beings. The intuitive method, in its pure and original conceptualization, gives exclusive relevance to learning processes and mechanisms that are based solely on non-analytical and nonrational components, and see emotional, sensorial, and empathic perceptions as the protagonists of the human experience for both individuals and societies. In this field, that approach has inevitably caused, in many cases, to dismiss too quickly or superficially the actual importance of rational thinking based on logical axioms and conclusions reached through the scientific method.

Western psychotherapy and psychiatry alone do not take into consideration enough the wellbeing of an individual as a whole, in his physical and spiritual components, and are generally based on deductive reasoning, i.e., theories that move from broader generalizations to specific observations. The deductive method is normally used to test existing theories rather than develop new ones. In the field of psychotherapy and psychiatry, this approach has inevitably caused a vast categorization and a sort of bureaucratic inclination by psychotherapists to force their patients into labels, definitions, or categories without regard for personal and subjective characteristics.

That is why I have dedicated more than 20 years of my life to studying, researching, and developing a complete and thorough discipline for self-growth.

This discipline acknowledges and uses the most effective findings and techniques of Eastern and Western cultures, and it is also capable of surpassing their respective limitations, going beyond old conventions and mindsets to achieve the ultimate goal of one compelling and systematic approach.

I found the solution in integrative therapy. Its winning factor is that it is mostly based on inductive reasoning, i.e., theories that move from specific observations to broad generalizations, and that are normally used to develop new theories or evolve existing ones. The inductive method is regularly used whenever we need to focus on an individual and specific person, event, issue, or circumstance, and we record data and information in an analytical way so we can use our existing knowledge and experience to identify commonalities, patterns, or singularities.

In this field, the advantage of this approach is that it gives primary importance to understanding the subjective and personal characteristics of a person, their individual features, and treats them as a whole in order to build a profile that becomes the paradigm of the future analysis.

Once there is that paradigm in place, we can search among Eastern and Western reservoirs of methods and techniques to find the ones that best fit the needs and interests of the individual, so we can provide convincing, solid, and durable answers and solutions to whatever the topic or issue might be.

The challenge Integrative Therapy poses is not an easy task because it requires a different effort from the counselor's side and from the side of the person seeking counseling.

The counselor needs to embrace a multi-disciplinary approach, be willing to enrich their knowledge from different sources, commit the required time to explore each person's case properly, and develop a method tailored to the individual.

The person seeking counseling or support needs to be receptive and open-minded about the possible sources from which the answer to their problems, obstacles, and issues may come from. They need to accept that the solution resides within their Self and requires an evolution that might be uncomfortable at times, but that will be extremely beneficial.

I can guarantee you that the rewards the Integrative Therapy approach can offer are incredibly positive, constructive, and effective.

Integrative Therapy. What is it? How does it work? Why does it work?

Integrative therapy aims to favor healing and to achieve wholeness, ensuring that all levels of a person's being and functioning (mental, physical, and emotional health) are maximized to their full potential. On the other end, the individual must be committed to self-exploration and open to identifying what factors in their life are perpetuating problems and/or are causing current concerns.

In particular, the integrative approach helps people face each moment openly and authentically without having formed an opinion, expectation, or attitude beforehand. This enables them to better focus on the fears and hurts that limit their psychological freedom and recognize specific triggers that may be causing disruptive patterns of behavior.

Through this awareness, integrative therapy helps create a healthy synergy between mind and body, empowering us to start setting goals and practicing new behaviors that will enable us to move beyond our limitations and discover greater life satisfaction.

The counselor's role within the integrative approach is to cater to each person's therapeutic experience by using specific techniques and key concepts drawn from various methods, all of which are deemed appropriate for the individual and their needs.

Integrative Therapy is a new, more contemporary approach in which the affective, cognitive, behavioral, and physiological systems within a person are brought together, and a special attention is dedicated to the awareness of the social and transpersonal aspects of the systems surrounding the person. Integrative therapy aims to facilitate wholeness and to maximize the quality of the person's being and functioning in the intra-cognitive, interpersonal, and social space while regarding each individual's limits and external constraints.

Why is this important? Because to find real purpose and meaning in life, we need the skill to discern which events occur to us caused by other people or circumstances, and which ones are instead rooted in behaviors we are responsible for: ultimately, it is a matter of accountability.

In this regard, the words of Carl Jung, the renowned "Father of Modern Analytical Psychology," still potently resonates these days: "The psychological rule says that when an inner situation is not made conscious, it happens outside, as fate. That is to say, when the individual remains undivided and does not become conscious of his inner contradictions, the world must perforce act out the conflict and be torn into opposite halves."[1]

In a nutshell, when an inner situation or state (feeling, emotion, sensation, belief, etc.) is not made conscious, it appears outside of you as fate. Suppose we don't pay attention, analyze, and try to understand the sources, dynamics, and outcomes of our unconscious and subconscious. In that case, we will live thinking and believing that "things," especially the bad ones, simply happen to us.

Therefore, we usually blame destiny, fate, good or bad luck, other people, God, and random circumstances. And sometimes it is true that there are a series of factors, encounters, and events that are entirely outside our control-sphere or extemporaneous.

But it is even 'more' true and compelling to recognize that in most cases, and for the most part, what happens to us - and what we cause to happen - have their roots in our unconscious and subconscious. Therefore, we are the cause of the events that 'happen' to us.

Unconscious and subconscious are the engines of which we are, by definition, only partially or completely not aware of.

In other words, both the unconscious mind and the subconscious mind heavily and firmly determine our behaviors and route us in all sorts of decisions and reactions we manifest, and they set us up in all the aspects of our lives. Yet, we are not 'aware' of their actual load on our behavior.

---

[1] Aion: Researches into the Phenomenology of the Self by C.G. Jung

We do not acknowledge the real influence they have on our lives because it all happens without being detected by the radar of the conscious mind, which is structured to give us the impression, sometimes the illusion, that we are always in control.

At first, it is natural to feel unsettled and disoriented at the thought that inside us, there are powerful forces (unconscious and subconscious) that so widely determine what happens in our lives, but of which we are not cognizant of. And it might lead us to think that the notion of 'control' itself is an illusion, that our decisions are inherently affected and contaminated by unaware causes.

Are we simply a stalk of grass at the mercy of natural elements? Puppets, manipulated by the dark recesses of our mind? Is life itself a lie?

The answer is no.

Our conscious mind is - indeed - the most powerful tool we have to grab the reins of our life and intervene in our unconscious and subconscious to maximize the control of what happens to us by being in unison with our thoughts and emotions.

And there is no better tool to analyze and understand the streams of our thoughts and emotions than the Ladder of Inference, the model that allows us to understand how our consciousness works and which we will study later in Part I - Chapter 2.

The purpose of the book 'Life is a Treasure Hunt'

Thanks to this book, I have been finally able to organize my knowledge and experience as an intuitive coach and integrative counselor and instill them in a tested and proven method that can help anyone who wants to tackle in life what is holding them back, keeping them away from achieving their goals, so they can ultimately become experts on how to win challenges and become better versions of themselves.

My method is based on my techniques Integrative Identity Development System™ and Seven Tools for the Treasure Hunt™.

The Integrative Identity Development System™ that I apply in my practice is about how to run and achieve Introspection through the Enhanced Ladder of Inference (see Part I - Chapter 3).

The Seven Tools for the Treasure Hunt™ that I also apply in my practice is about how to discover and master our innate Spirit of Adventure with practical mindsets and behaviors (see Part II).

Combined, the Integrative Identity Development System™ and the Seven Tools for the Treasure Hunt™ offer the chance to reach Higher Consciousness, the ultimate tool to live a purposeful and meaningful life.

The essential steps in this discipline are very clear and straightforward:
- Integrative Therapy is the most effective way to reach deep and conscious Introspection.
- Introspection is the most effective way to find and unlock our Spirit of Adventure, discover, and achieve Self-awareness.

- Introspection and Spirit of Adventure are the foundation and structural pillar of Higher Consciousness because they enable working on the unconscious and subconscious, so that the conscious behavior and decision-making are aligned with growth, betterment, purpose, success, fulfillment.

And Consciousness is going to be the topic of the second chapter of this book.

My Introduction

By Deborah Sanguineti

I first met Joseph in early 2019. I was curating an art exhibition in New York City, where the gallery's owner introduced us. We agreed to meet and discuss his potential involvement in my upcoming exhibit, and two hours went by in the blink of an eye. We covered so many topics! Needless to say, I was very impressed by his wealth of knowledge. Fortunately, he did play an important role in the exhibition, and two years later, here we are, having collaborated on this book.

He introduced me to the idea that "Life is a Treasure Hunt," sharing what he had been studying for over 20 years. We talked about who could benefit from this. As a woman in her 50s, I hoped it would appeal to women in this age range and older who may (wrongly) feel that their best years were behind them. As a mother of one college student and one recent graduate, I hoped it would help them take on the challenges of their uncertain futures. And I hoped it would appeal to anyone considering changing their career, making a personal decision, or contemplating a fresh start - yet being held back by fear and uncertainty.

With this book, I began my own "search for the Treasure" as I spent countless hours reflecting on past journeys - those taken and NOT taken - and the tools I had and those I didn't. I needed to do the work to understand and acquire each tool to complete this particular journey. Once the book was finished and I collected my treasure, I understood how powerful this process had been for me personally and professionally, and how powerful it could be for others.

An important discovery made was learning about the Ladder of Inference, particularly the enhanced version Joseph developed. Prior to this experience, I never gave much thought to our conscious, subconscious, and unconscious. Sure, I would throw these words around, but they were still just words. I never considered the information they held and the power they had. As it will be discussed in the following chapters of this book, change happens, but life, for the most part, doesn't simply happen. We have more control than we believe when we think that life (supposedly) simply happens, but our subconscious and unconscious have stored information we are not aware of (and in some cases, prefer it that way), which could derail us from understanding that when we allow for introspection, we can release some of that information and make it useful for our own causes.

A personal example with regards to writing this book was the following: consciously, I wanted to accept the challenge of writing it; subconsciously, I needed to maintain a positive working relationship with Joseph. I reflected on past partnerships and made a checklist of why some succeeded, and some didn't. This one would include respect, patience, and accountability, as well as having to check myself a few times. Lastly, I think my unconscious was somehow drawn to such a topic because my impulse led me to take on the challenge. I felt I wanted to attain that higher level of consciousness

Joseph shared with me. When I finished writing this book, I understood why this happened through a lot of thoughtful introspection. It wasn't simply fate that Joseph asked me to co-write this book. It was how we had interacted and communicated when we met because of the art exhibition. A connection was made, we stayed in touch, and over a year later, a book began. I think about how we communicated, and I pushed myself to keep it healthy and respectful because THIS was something I could control.

Your subconscious and unconscious can be pretty helpful, essential even, in helping you be more mindful, more in control of your own feelings, more balanced, and less surprised when life "just happens." Once I untapped this, the Enhanced Ladder of Inference made perfect sense because it is made up of our very own personalities and beliefs, which are found - you guessed it - in our conscious, subconscious, and unconscious.

The Enhanced Ladder of Inference (see Chapter 3) explains something we do every day, throughout the entire day: we make decisions. It is a real eye-opener to realize that the smallest decisions, as well as the most important ones, go through that 7-step process, but they do. I will share my own personal example in chapter 3, but for now think about decisions you have made that started with just the facts, and because of your preferences or beliefs, or because of what was hiding in your subconscious or unconscious, the situation ended as it did. Maybe it was an unrecognized fear of change that kept you from doing something, allowing it to control you instead of you controlling it.

Writing this book has undoubtedly influenced my belief system forever. I see things differently now, past and present, and I go about doing things differently because of this: your actions and how you communicate are rooted in "something," and that something is your subconscious and unconscious.

The tools you will go after will help you find your treasure step by step. This isn't a marathon. It's a journey - your journey. Now, let's go after it!

PART I

CHAPTER 1

Your Consciousness is your Superpower

The central and fundamental theme of the present book is to comprehend and strengthen Higher Consciousness. What is it? Why do we need it? How do we achieve it and use it?

The answer starts with the realization that changes happen. They are inevitable. Sometimes we are aware of them; some others, we are not. Changes can occur from the inside, when our unconscious, subconscious or conscious mind determines them, or from the outside, when determined by nature, people, or external situations.

We instinctively fear change because it imbalances our stability. And we value stability, order, routine because we find comfort in them.

Higher Consciousness is the element that allows us to take control of our life and its outcome. Why? How?

What I implement in this book and guide you to do is to break down Consciousness into Introspection and Spirit of Adventure.

Introspection allows us to train and use our Higher Consciousness to influence and drive our unconscious and subconscious, those levels of the mind that have a tremendous impact on our reasoning and behavior but of which we usually have only a little or no awareness of. After all, if we look at the Latin etymology of the words, 'subconscious' literally means 'below awareness' and 'unconscious' 'absence of awareness.'

The traditional explanation of the three general levels of the mind follows the structure below:
- Consciousness defines our thoughts, actions, and awareness.
- Subconscious is defined as the actions and reactions we realize when we think of them.
- Unconscious is defined as the set of deeper mental processes encompassing a reservoir of feelings, thoughts, urges, and memories outside of our conscious awareness.

An example to better understand how these three levels work can be a very common daily activity we are all engaged with: talking over our cellphone while walking.
- Consciousness determines our voluntary action: I am talking
- Subconscious determines our Carried-along action: breathing and walking while talking, but also feelings, emotions, and thoughts as a response to the topic or tone of the conversation
- Unconscious determines our Involuntary action: I dial the wrong number or say the wrong name in my conversation (events usually referred to as Freudian slips), or instinctive reactions as response to the topic or tone of the conversation.

Traditional approaches in psychology and psychiatry tend to depict the unconscious and subconscious almost as unstoppable forces or invariable traits of our mind and connote consciousness generally as a 'low-intensity' level of the mind. According to those approaches, as human beings, we spend most of our lives functioning in states of lower consciousness, where what we are principally concerned with is ourselves, our survival, and our own success, strictly defined, and only in specific situations or circumstances we experience states of higher consciousness. And that system is basically presented as a status quo we can study and analyze but barely change.

Introspection through my Integrative Identity Development System™, instead, puts Higher Consciousness at the center of the human experience, as a force that - over time - can effectively mold the subconscious and even counter or channel the impulses coming from the unconscious if adequately trained and supported.

The second component or structural element of Higher Consciousness I mentioned earlier in this chapter, and in the Introduction, is the Spirit of Adventure.

The Spirit of Adventure allows us to tame our fears and embrace the changes that occur to us, and it is the innate force we need in order to learn how to unlock and let emerge it so that it can inform our decisions and behaviors.

And the system I developed through The Seven Tools for the Treasure Hunt™ has precisely the purpose of providing a checklist and guidelines on how to let your Spirit of Adventure unfold and lead you to find your way to live a purposeful and meaningful life.

The Integrative Therapy approach discussed in the Introduction has the merit to give Consciousness the importance and decisiveness it deserves. Higher Consciousness is the key to achieve Self-Awareness. Self-Awareness leads to Self-Realization and Wellness.

Mastering our Higher Consciousness allows us to find the Meaning of Life. That's why it is our very own Superpower.

CHAPTER 2

The Ladder of Inference: the traditional approach

The Ladder of Inference is a model first developed and presented by Harvard Professor Chris Argyris in the early '70s and that reached popularity when it appeared in the publication by Peter Senge's 'The Fifth Discipline: The Art and Practice of the Learning Organization' published in 1994.

The model breaks down and describes the mental processes that take place in our brain every time we go from observation to assessment to action. It is something we do thousands of times every day, and that it is involved in the simplest tasks we perform as well as the most complicated ones.

Ordinarily, the process happens in a split second, almost instantaneously. It is so embedded, well-oiled, and familiar that we perceive it as automatic, natural, spontaneous. But it is not.

The ladder of inference, which we can also call the sequence of inference, is the process our conscious mind follows for decision making, it takes place in the present moment, and it's the pattern in which the seven tools we will discuss further in this book take place.

The Ladder of Inference - The traditional model

Finish

7 Taking Action — 7. Take action based on our adjusted beliefs [Action(s)]

6 Adjusting Beliefs — 6. Adjust beliefs (about the world around us – including person or people involved in the experience of the moment) [Adjusting]

5 Conclusions — 5. Conclusions (based on our assumptions – creation of emotional reactions) [Conclusions]

4 Assuming — 4. Assumptions (based on the meaning as we interpreted it– overlapping of what is facts and what is story) [Assumptions]

3 Interpretation — 3. Assign meaning (starting to interpret what information tell us) [Interpreted Reality – Interpreting facts]

2 Filtering — 2. Filter Info (tendencies, preferences etc.) [Selected Reality – Selecting]

1 Raw Data — 1. Raw data and observations of our experience (experience of the moment) [Reality and Facts - Observations]

Start

When we engage in a situation, either actively or passively, the sequence below shows us how our brain works.

Let's picture the sequence of inference as a ladder with seven rungs; from bottom to top, we have 1) observation of raw data, 2) filtering observed data, 3) assigning meaning to the filtered information, 4) making assumptions based on the meaning assigned, 5) reaching conclusions based on the assumptions, 6) adjusting our beliefs according to the conclusions we reached, 7) taking action according to our beliefs.

An incisive parameter we can use to understand this process better is the level of objectivity and subjectivity involved in each step of the sequence or rung of the ladder.

At the bottom rung - raw data and its observation - the level of objectivity is maximal, and the level of subjectivity is minimal: we are looking exclusively at facts, pure and simple factual elements and circumstances without any personal, individual, subjective involvement whatsoever.

At the top rung instead - taking action - the level of objectivity is minimal, and the level of subjectivity is maximal: we are looking exclusively at our personal and individual action taken according to our subjective beliefs with no connections anymore to the original factual situation. Instead, we have just created a new reality as a consequence of our behavior.

The second to the sixth, the intermediate rungs (or steps of the sequence), gradually go from a higher level to a lower level of objectivity and from a lower level to a higher level of subjectivity.

The turning point occurs between rung three and four when we make assumptions based on the meaning we assigned to the previously filtered facts. We will examine the details of this transition when we focus on the respective steps of the sequence.

What is described above is the railway on which our decision-making process travels; it is a straightforward, one-way path from facts to actions.

Let's break it down rung by rung (step by step).

1) Observation of raw data (Observation)

At the first stage of the sequence, or the bottom rung of the ladder according to the analogy we are using, we find the observation of raw data. That means that when we face an occurrence in our life, at the very beginning, we are simply immersed in the reality around us, and we are mere observers, like a cameraman recording a video. So, we simply look at and watch the people, the objects, and the circumstances we are surrounded by.

2) Filtering observed data (Filtering)

At the second stage of the sequence, or the second rung of the ladder, we find ourselves filtering the data we are observing, and as a filter, we first and foremost use our attention and focus on the priorities dictated by factual circumstances, our tendencies, preferences, inclinations, taste, and previous experiences. This is the stage in which the outside world enters our inner world, and we start processing the information and select it.

The objective reality outside us begins to be internalized inside us, and our subjectivity peeps out, and like a sieve, we use it to comb through all the available information to sort the ones we deem relevant according to, again, factual circumstances, our tendencies, preferences, inclinations, taste, and previous experiences.

3) Assigning meaning to the filtered information (Interpreting)

At the third stage of the sequence, or the third rung of the ladder, we assign meaning to the information we have previously filtered, and the way we do it is through what we commonly call interpretation. Therefore, at this stage, the level of objectivity keeps decreasing while the level of subjectivity increases and gradually begins to take over.

The action of interpretating consists in explaining the meaning of something; its etymology derives from the Latin *interpretatio* (explanation, exposition). More properly, we can state that the action of interpreting is the sum or synthesis of three actions: explaining, expounding, and understanding. The result that we achieve through them is that our consciousness assigns a meaning to facts it already observed and filtered over the previous phases.

4) Making assumptions based on the meaning assigned (Assuming)

At the fourth stage of the sequence, or the fourth rung of the ladder, the decisive turning point from objectivity to subjectivity that we mentioned earlier occurs. We make our assumption based not on the objective facts and circumstances of a situation but on the interpretation, the version, the meaning we assigned to those facts and circumstances.

This is a phase of pivotal importance because it is when our conscious mind moves from the factual aspect of reality and starts the <u>narration</u> of the facts to its own self: the line between what is 'facts' and what is 'story' becomes blurred in our consciousness, and we start to apply our character with an intensity capable of bending, molding, shaping the external reality to give it the form we want.

From this point on, in our decision-making process, we use the tale, the recounting of the facts and circumstances told to our Self by our own mind after the latter has observed, selected, and interpreted them. In other words, at this stage, we have a sub-product of reality, one elaborated for the most part by our subjectivity. As a consequence, a much less broad spectrum of factors falls into consideration, and much more relevance we give to personal and individual components for the determination of the subsequent steps of the sequence.

5) Reaching conclusions based on the assumptions (Conclusions)

At the fifth stage of the sequence, or the fifth rung of the ladder, a decisive step is taken by our conscious mind, which has now reached a new plateau that can be used as a base, a ground solid enough to support the structure built by our subjectivity and get to the end of its path.

That step is: drawing the conclusion based on the assumptions determined in the previous phase of the sequence.

At this point, our personal, individual, subjective traits have absolved their purpose since they have fulfilled the task of shaping a complete story of the events and circumstances initially observed. A story, a recounting that is entirely 'ours' because we have filtered it, interpreted it, and understood it according to the way we are. Our conscious mind in this phase utilizes a version, an account of the reality that was molded by its assumptions, presuppositions, and prejudices, and it is what resolves and determines our Self to take the conclusive step of drawing the conclusions it needs before taking actual action.

The takeover by our subjectivity over objectivity is almost complete since we have concluded the internalization and 'personalization' of the situation we are in, and we are ready to do what we want to do. We need one more step before triggering the impulse that causes our behavior.

6) Adjusting our beliefs according to the conclusions we reached (Adjusting beliefs)

At the sixth stage of the sequence, or the 6th rung of the ladder, an interesting phenomenon occurs that is partially counter-intuitive. In this phase, we adjust our beliefs and convictions according to the experience of the present moment (the one that started the climbing of the ladder) and the conclusions we reached in the previous phase. Common knowledge would lead us to false logic: we might think that we check and corroborate our beliefs before, and not after, drawing our conclusions. But that is not the case.

As a matter of fact, the way our decision-making process works is that first, we reach certain conclusions, then compare them with our system of beliefs and convictions. Lastly, we regulate, adapt, adjust those beliefs and convictions on the basis of the experience of the present moment and to validate and reinforce the conclusions we already reached. In other words, our conscious mind uses our present stances and opinions to determine a conclusion and only afterward runs a final and ultimate comparison with our creeds, values, principles, and worldviews before taking actual action.

7) Taking action according to our beliefs (Taking Action)

At the seventh stage of the sequence, or the top rung of the ladder, our consciousness takes action according to, and consistently with, our beliefs and convictions.

Our decision-making process reaches its end, and the product of our consciousness goes from our inner world to the world outside: this is a very powerful moment because it is when we intervene and have an influence on the reality as it was at the beginning of the process, and we change it with our actions. At this stage, we create and determine a different, new reality, a new situation that is the product, the consequence of our action(s).

We have come full circle: we started the process in the external world, and we return back to it with an action that can be active or passive, or that can be by doing or by omission, or, last but not least, that can be aggressive or submissive. In all these scenarios we are going to influence the initial situation one way or another, and we're going to determine a new one.

Joseph R. Fraia

CHAPTER 3

Enhanced Ladder of Inference: the new version developed by the Integrative Identity Development System™

In the previous chapter, we saw the traditional model of the Ladder of Inference and how our Conscious Mind works according to the conventional approach of classic psychology and neuropsychology. With its clarity and simplicity, it is an extraordinary model that shows us the hard science behind our Conscious Mind and how our decision-making process actually works. It also offers a structure we can trust as a source of comparison every time we need to make a particularly important decision, as a sort of checklist or operating manual we can refer to when we want to ponder the pertinence, accuracy, and suitability of a decision from which we wish or expect a favorable outcome.

Thanks to Integrative Therapy, though, it is possible to contribute enriching and to enhance an already excellent tool, and show an even more complete and thoroughgoing picture of the frame of our Consciousness, and the full process that takes place in our subjective experience of the objective world. As usual, understanding how something works puts us in the best position to become better at it, and how to evolve and improve it.

That is how we can become experts of ourselves and use Introspection to unlock our Spirit of Adventure.

Through the Integrative Identity Development System™ that I apply in my sessions, workshops, and seminars, and that I outline in this book, I can present the Enhanced version of the Ladder of Inference I have enhanced it by implementing the concepts of Floor, Ceiling and Reflective Loop + Action Loop as features that enable us to better understand, influence and shape our unconscious and subconscious and increase control over our conscious behaviors and actions.

The Enhanced Ladder of Inference

Ceiling

The Ceiling is made by the results of our actions, creates a new experience, and generates two loops: The Reflective Loop and the Action Loop.

The Reflective Loop: the new experience will influence our belief system and what data we select next time.

The Action Loop: the new experience creates and represents new situations, new behaviors, new choices.

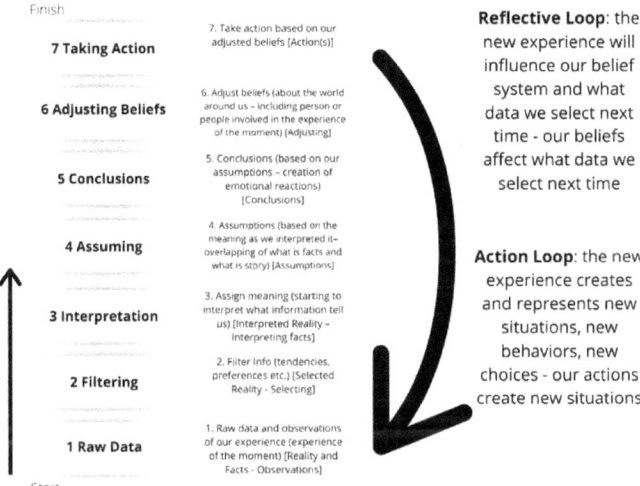

Floor

The Floor is made by the real physical world around us AND our current existing personality and beliefs' system (experience).

Our personality and beliefs system have three layers: the surface (visible) is the Conscious, the underlying (covered) is the Subconscious, and the buried (not visible) is the Unconscious.

How the Enhanced Ladder of Inference works and why it's great for You

Here follows how the Enhanced Ladder of Inference works:
Below the first rung at the bottom, we have the Floor.
The Floor is made by the real physical world around us and our current existing personality and beliefs' system: in other words, our character and the sum of our experiences so far.
As we saw in the previous chapters, our personality and beliefs system have three layers: the surface (visible) is the Conscious, the underlying (covered) is the Subconscious, and the buried (not visible) is the Unconscious. These three strata encompass our inner wholeness and are the ground on which we set our ladder every time we make a decision.

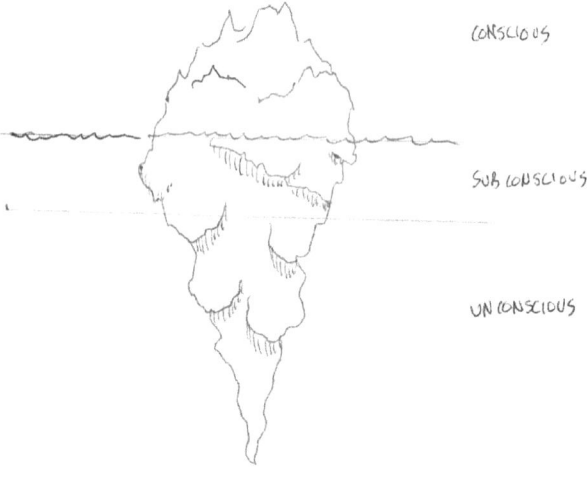

Above the seventh rung at the top, we have the Ceiling, which is made by the results of our actions, creates a new experience, and generates two loops: the Reflective Loop and the Action Loop.

The Reflective Loop is the set of new knowledge and experience that will influence our belief system and what data we select next time.

The Action Loop is the set of new knowledge and experience that creates and represents new situations, new behaviors, new choices.

The sum of the Reflective Loop, the Action Loop and the Ceiling creates a New Floor, that is going to be the ground for the next ladder of inference.

In other words, on top of the seventh rung (Take action), the Ceiling becomes a new experience which then becomes the new floor for the next ladder to be climbed.

Another great advantage of this model is that it makes very clear the spiral structure of our decision-making and learning processes and highlights the direct and remarkable benefits we can obtain when that spiral goes upward. Because we become aware of those processes, and we can use them to improve our control over our instincts and intellect, creativity and knowledge, for a real betterment of our Self.

But the same model also warns us of the danger of that spiral going downward, which happens when we keep ignoring how that model works and don't get control over it, or we limit ourselves to simply witness the dynamics played by the unconscious and subconscious without channeling them, so inevitably our decision-making process remains or becomes mutable, eccentric, unstable and incoherent. Or even worse, our values and beliefs stay or become stiff, narrow-minded, egocentric and intolerant.

Instead, the comforting and uplifting action that derives from the awareness and the control over the Enhanced Ladder of Inference is that we actively participate in building our personality and character, we can both better compare and assess our values and beliefs, and more effectively direct them towards our desired goals and the purpose of living a full and meaningful life.

Once - thanks to the Integrative Identity Development System™ - we have a clear and complete understanding of the cycle Floor (conscious, subconscious, unconscious), Ladder (enhanced ladder of inference), Ceiling (reflective loop and active loop), New Floor (result of experience) then we can tackle the worst and most dangerous enemy of humankind: Fear. The protagonist of our next chapter.

Joseph R. Fraia

My Enhanced Ladder of Inference

In my introduction, I touched upon Joseph's Enhanced Ladder of Inference. My story goes like this.

One morning, my son decided to take the semester off due to Covid online classes. He came to me and shared his thoughts. The fact was that I needed to understand his point of view, why he thought the way he did, and I purposely reached out for a Higher Consciousness assessment as a parent. I had two possible options, either support him or not. My spontaneous and natural reaction was to, in fact, support him. My assumption was that it was a smart and healthy decision based on what the last two semesters were like for him. I concluded this was the best choice for him and his state of mind. If he was at ease, I, as a parent, would be more at ease. I also concluded that my son would benefit from the break as his plan entailed going out West to live with a friend, work at a ski resort, and get some skiing in. I took out my credit card, paid for his flights, but told him the rest of the expenses were on him. He had a wonderful experience, embraced his "spirit of adventure", and is now registered for Fall classes.

With the Ladder of Inference, *enhanced* by Integrative Therapy," the floor was my decision-making process based on my personal feelings about my son's well-being, preferring he has a break from Covid and "live a little". The ceiling was when I gave him the biggest hug before he headed for the airport.

From the ceiling, two loops were generated. The Reflexive Loop was listening to my son's reasons for taking a semester off from college and helping him prepare for the trip out West, based on my belief that it would be more impactful than spending his days on a computer and not getting the support he counts on. Then came the Action Loop, where I accepted his plan with the condition of he finding a job and me letting him go. Letting him go created a new situation for me, and see how he will have handled himself would have created a new experience for me. If he either would have stayed out West or returned to school it would set for me a new floor, waiting for the next loops to go around again.

Deborah Sanguineti

CHAPTER 4

Break the bars of your invisible cage

Change is inevitable, and most of the time is not under our control. On top of that, change determines an instinctive and automatic discomfort in us, a feeling that can quickly deteriorate in fear, panic, and inaction. But we can overcome that discomfort and the Fear of Change using our Introspection and Spirit of Adventure to live a meaningful and purposeful life.

How do we interiorize and metabolize this essential truth? How do we take this statement and relate to it? How can we bend our willpower and drive our actions towards this goal?

Because words by themselves are not enough. We wish it were possible to simply read something we need to do and automatically behave accordingly, like installing a software in a computer or an app on our phone. But we, as humans, do not work that way.

We need to understand. We need something to make sense to us. We need to feel that something is worth pursuing and achieving. It is the constructive side of our nature, the 'can-do' attitude, and it is the sparkle that keeps us alive and alert, motivated and resourceful. We can call this approach the 'Spirit of Adventure.'

But the exact nature of ours also has a dismantling side, the 'can't-do' attitude, the weight that makes us slower and unproductive, discouraged and inactive. We can call it 'The Fear of Change.' Our worst enemy, because it is insidious, subtle, astute, deceitful, and most of the time undetected by our consciousness.

By contrast, we can say that the above-mentioned 'Spirit of Adventure' is the attitude, the mindset by which we actually *welcome* change instead of fear it.

It is the approach that allows us to set ourselves open and ready to embrace the new and uncharted ahead of us. It is the sparkle that ignites our initiatives, even when we are aware that what awaits us is partially or entirely unknown. Yet, we determine ourselves to go for it anyway.

When that happens, it's because we either feel we have the skills to control and handle whatever the future holds for us, or we assess it as worth taking the chance. The new status quo resulting from the change might be better than the one we are currently in.

The Fear of Change is the nemesis of the Spirit of Adventure. It is the force that does not allow the sparkle of initiative to get lit up and, at the same time, freezes our actions, setting up our immobility towards the inevitable changes our life puts in front of us.

The time is ripe to finally tackle the 'Fear of Change.'

A cage with invisible bars

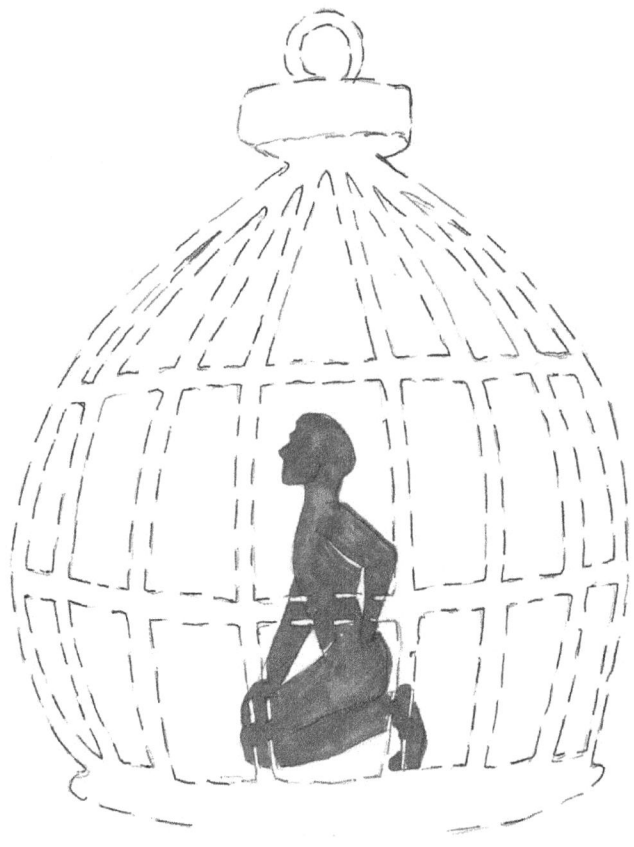

We can picture the Fear of Change as a cage with invisible bars: we are locked in and blocked, and we are not even aware of it. We think, we believe we are free when in reality, we are captives. It is a profoundly unsettling perspective, living a life with the illusion of being free when, in reality, we were prisoners all along.

But if the Fear of Change is this invisible and astute enemy that sneaks under our skin and takes over our actions, and we do not even realize its existence or presence, how do we fight it? How can we possibly win against it?

Well, that is a very good question, indeed, but it can be answered. We can fight and defeat our Fear of Change.

Change

To win over the Fear of Change, we need to break down its meaning and understand what causes it.

Let's start with the word 'Change.'

What is change?

As a verb, change can be defined as 'making the form, nature, content, future course, etc., of something different from what it is or what it would be if left alone.'

As a noun, change can be defined as 'a transformation or modification; alteration, a variation or deviation, *the passing from one place, state, form, or phase to another.*'

Hence in its essence, 'Change' is the passage from a condition to a *different* one.

So far, everything sounds pretty immediate and falls into what we usually call common knowledge. But we can do better than that.

So, let's dig a little bit deeper. Shall we?

According to the broad definitions we saw above, we perceive 'change' *only because* we pass from a previous state to the following one that is different: therefore, on a more philosophical level, we can say that 'change' happens only when we move from a preceding *status quo* to an ensuing *status quo*, from an *old* stable condition to a *new* stable condition. And that is why we can visualize 'change' as an eternal cycle: stability → change → stability → change, and so on.

Established anthropology and evolutionary behavior studies tell us that human beings normally find comfort in stability and discomfort in instability.

This reaction origins in the *archipallium*, or reptile brain, which includes the brain stem and the cerebellum: from the time we were primates and cave dwellers, we could immediately and intuitively perceive the advantages of safely remaining in a cave, repaired from natural elements and hungry predators, and the disadvantages of taking the chance, the risk of leaving that same cave and exposing ourselves to hostile weather and dangerous animals of prey.

There are, of course, many and various other reasons and nuances involved in the above-mentioned process, but they transcend and go beyond the scope and range of this book.

What we can do to move forward this line of reasoning is to focus on the results and conclusions provided by the scientific community on the topic of why we find comfort in stability, order, and safety while we find discomfort in instability, disorder, and vulnerability.

That phenomenon initially occurs in our unconscious and subconscious and falls into what we call 'instinct,' a natural or innate impulse, inclination, or tendency.

Ordinarily, we associate the idea of 'instinct' with the idea of 'automatism'. Given a fact or event, our immediate primary reaction is an instinctive, automatic one, after which we process the same fact or event with our rationality and consciousness.

Our very nature and primordial mechanism are the cause of the basic and fundamental attitude of preferring stability or the *absence of change* and disliking instability, the passage from a previous status quo to an ensuing status quo.

As human beings, we are inherently adverse towards change.

Keep that in mind for later as we now tackle the other protagonist of the 'Fear of Change.' Fear itself.

Fear

'Fear' is defined as a distressing emotion aroused by impending danger, evil, pain, etc., whether the threat is real or imagined, and as the feeling or condition of being afraid.

We can define 'fear' as an elementary, intense emotion triggered by the detection of an imminent threat, causing an immediate alarm reaction that mobilizes the organism by provoking a set of physiological changes that include rapid heartbeat, redirection of blood flow away from peripheral parts toward internal organs, tensing of the muscles, and a general aptitude of the organism to take action.

From the simple definitions of 'Fear,' we can point out its most peculiar feature: the **threat** that causes fear can be either **real or imagined,** but in both cases, our reaction is the same, has the same intensity, hence is equally **real**, and it is both physiological and behavioral.

Therefore, a danger that we might picture exclusively in our mind, even if entirely hypothetical, has the power to cause an effect in our physical, material world. And that is the real power of Fear.

But we have also learned that Fear is an emotion that **we** create and therefore are responsible for. Different external and internal factors might trigger it, yet you generate the emotional reaction that ensues. To an extent we can go as far as to say that fear starts as an instinct, but immediately after becomes a choice. And that is the key factor we were looking for.

We clarified earlier that Change simply happens, and we have little or limited control over it. But Fear, instead, is **entirely under our control**. Yes, its ignition might be almost automatic in reaction to a change, but it is entirely on us to either extinguish it or let it fire up.

That is the counter-intuitive but fundamental truth we need to internalize and own.

We grow up with the belief that we have or can have total control over our life's events (changes) and very little control of our emotions (fear). In contrast, the reality is precisely the opposite.

I want you to pause for a few minutes and really think about what we have just stated because the next step will baffle you even more. When you are ready, turn the page.

A. Master your fears to master your reality

Deep Introspection through the Integrative Identity Development System™

We can summarize the conclusions we have reached so far as follows: we experience the 'Fear of Change' because instinctively (pushed by our unconscious and subconscious), we perceive change as a real or imaginary threat. That is our evolutionary biological response to either the comfort that predictable stability (order) gives us, or the discomfort that unpredictable disorder (unknown) brings to us.

We have minimal control over what happens around us and to us, but we have extensive and direct control over our instincts, emotions, and thoughts.

And that fact might sound counter-intuitive, but it is the truth and it is an eye-opener. Since we have more control over our instincts, emotions, and thoughts than on our changes, we should direct our efforts and energies in controlling the former (instincts/emotions/thoughts) rather than the latter (changes).

And if among our instincts we tackle particularly the Fear of Change, something new, unexpected but magnificent happens: the more we control and master our fears, the more control we gain over the changes in our lives.

In other words, we can actually expand and increase our control over the events in our life if we increase our control over our emotions.

More importantly, we understand that Fear DOES NOT have to be the automatic or inevitable reaction to change. *Au contraire*: we can actually flip our emotional response to change and **embrace** it rather than fear it.

Introspection achieved through the Integrative Identity Development System™ is the key to suppress our 'Fear of Change' and ignite our 'Spirit of Adventure.'

B. Embrace change and take action - Ignite your Spirit of Adventure with The Seven Tools for the Treasure Hunt™

In the Introduction of this book, we have stressed that Higher Consciousness is the key to obtaining Self-Awareness, which can help us to achieve Wellness.

Higher Consciousness is a stage and a status in which we are aware of how our unconscious and subconscious work along with our knowledge, willpower, thoughts, and actions.

We clarified that Higher Consciousness has two faces, one that looks inward, Introspection, and the other outward, Spirit of Adventure.

In the previous Chapter, we went over again about how the Integrative Identity Development System™ - through the Enhanced Ladder of Inference - effectively performs the Introspection we need to influence our unconscious and subconscious so we can control our emotions and defeat Fear.

Now it is time to focus on the Spirit of Adventure to better understand what it is, how it works, and how to obtain it.

The Spirit of Adventure is the force supported by our conscious mind and built on our knowledge, wisdom, and experience, which allows us to look at changes in our lives as opportunities and not threats, as thresholds we can pass through to achieve better self-awareness, and not as locked gates that keep us trapped.

It is the impetus that determines the transition from thought to action. We are all born with it, and, like many other features of our personalities, each one of us possesses it in different degrees and forms. Hence some of us have a better inclination, predisposition to let express that inner spirit; for some others, it requires more focus and dedication.

Nevertheless, to use the full potential of the Spirit of Adventure and benefit from its positive influence, everyone needs regular and compelling training or exercise. Like a muscle, regular workouts increase strength and make it easier to keep the shape and stay fit.

The knowledge of Introspection and of how the Enhanced Ladder of Inference works gives us the ability to understand and use the first of the Seven Tools for the Treasure Hunt™: Discovery.

And that is where Part II of this book starts.

Joseph R. Fraia

PART II

CHAPTER 1

Discovery

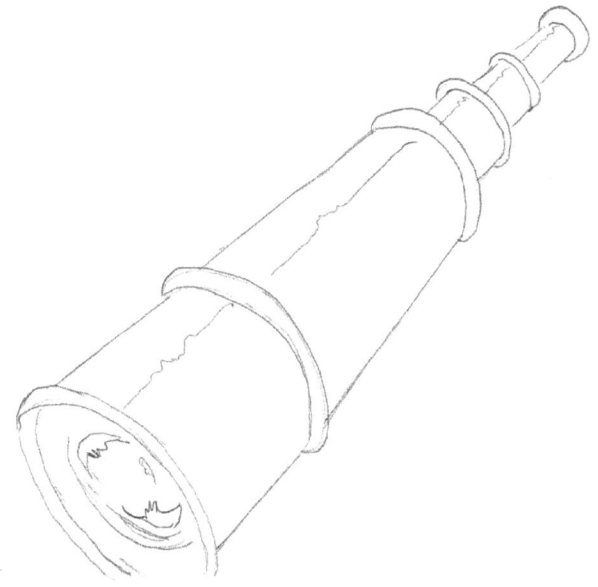

In the previous chapters, you have seen the advantages of taking control of your life by embracing your 'Spirit of Adventure' and taming the 'Fear of Change,' and also how useful it is to realize that. We weren't born ready, and we need to learn and master specific skills to complete our journey successfully.

We have used, for that purpose, the image of a toolbox set up with the best tools available to ensure the success of our quest.

The first and foundational tool we need is **Discovery**.

The **Discovery** is the revelation and fundamental realization of the necessity to be or become aware that changes in life are inevitable and, for the most part, out of our direct control. What we can control is, instead, how we prepare ourselves to face and respond to these changes and, ultimately, guide and handle the events that occur in our lives in the direction preferable and favorable to us.

In the previous chapters, we have seen that we can maximize that approach when we look at life as a journey, a quest, a hunt towards a great reward, the ultimate treasure, and when we manage and defeat our 'Fear of Change' while we nurture and develop our 'Spirit of Adventure'

How do I know if I already possess the Discovery tool or if I need to acquire and develop it?

The answer resides in our Higher Consciousness and the Self-Awareness we can reach through it.

a. First of all, it is fundamental to realize that safety, security, and stability are significant and even essential in life. Still, they are also inherently temporary and momentary.

It is easy to fall into the illusion that those conditions are permanent and stable. As a result, we grow the conviction and belief that safety, security, and stability are ought to us or that they belong to us as a right of nature. But that is not true. Instead, Change is the constant of the human condition, and Fear of change is most often what stops us from embracing it. The genuine and willful acceptance of this fundamental truth is the key element to make that fear disappear.

b. You know you possess the **Discovery** tool if at this moment in your life you feel either centered, grounded, or safe, secure, comfortable in your own skin; other signals are the feeling of belonging in this world, happy to be alive, or if you see yourself as trusting, independent and poised.

Usually, signs of the **Discovery** tool are the perception of ourselves as focused and determined, committed and willful to make sacrifices to achieve our goals. In addition, we feel healthy and in good spirit, with a positive and optimistic attitude, energized, and in good shape.

You can apply this tool in any area of your life: it can be a personal relationship, a career path, a family relation, choosing a school, college, or course of study. It can be a sport you practice or a discipline you follow, but it can also be a mistake you are trying to fix or wrongdoing you are trying to set straight.

You know you possess the **Discovery** tool when you have assessed a situation at your best. You have weighted the circumstances using your knowledge and experience. When those weren't sufficient, you resorted to consulting experts or getting coached on how to handle the situation best.

But you didn't stop there, and you determined yourself to take action and take matters into your own hands, accepting the risks and uncertainty surrounding the situation because you see a likely favorable outcome of your actions.

c. You know you haven't mastered the **Discovery** tool at the moment, or just yet, if you feel your energies are scattered, or if you're suffering from anxiety and you're blocked by the fear of change and/or the lack of control on your life.

Usually, signs of this condition are the continuous procrastination of errands, obligations, and responsibilities, lack of motivation, a general feeling of numbness, or behavioral disorders (eating, sleeping, lack of exercising).

We might have the sensation or impression that everything is ok in our life, until we are confronted with a specific situation, person, or choice, in which case we decide to steer direction away from it, avoid confrontation or simply ignore it.

It can be an issue at work, with a family member, with a partner, it can be the choice to start or drop a task or a career, to change or end a routine, to go to the doctor or a therapist, to lose weight or stop drinking or smoking.

Those above are examples of imbalances, or lack of balance, in our life, which ultimately has the result of depriving us of the **Discovery** tool.

The question then becomes: how can we detect and recognize that lack of balance?

d. Clear signs of the imbalance mentioned above are the feeling of being fearful, anxious, unsure, ungrounded, or held back despite your best intentions. In some other cases, you might experience frustration, lack of initiative, or the tendency to shy away from confrontations even when you know you are right.

On the one hand, you might also be experiencing financial instability or feel driven/dragged away by greed, lust for power, aggressiveness, materialism, cynicism.

On the other hand, you might feel unloved, overly dependent on others' judgment, love, attention, or feel sexually inadequate or dissatisfied.

As you can see, it is an extensive repertoire of red flags signaling that 'something is going on,' a list that we all know very well but also that we tend to ignore or overlook, and they all come down to one common origin: the lack of balance.

The typical result of these imbalances determines a very well-known phenomenon: 'to act out.'

The American Psychological Association Dictionary of Psychology defines 'acting out' as follows:

1. the behavioral expression of emotions that serves to relieve tension associated with these emotions or communicate them in a disguised or indirect way to others. Such behaviors may include arguing, fighting, stealing, threatening, or throwing tantrums.

2. in psychoanalytic theory, the reenactment of past events as an expression of unconscious emotional conflicts, feelings, or desires - often sexual or aggressive - with no conscious awareness of the origin or meaning of these behaviors.

Hence, in the psychology of defense mechanisms and self-control, acting out is the performance of an action considered bad or anti-social. In general usage, the action performed is destructive to self or to others.

How to solve the imbalances and regain stability

Realize that stability is temporary, change is inevitable, and, for the most part, not under our control.

What we can control is our attitude towards change.

Examine changes in your life through the lens of the Introspection we discussed in the previous Part I of the book and tell yourself that you are in control of your emotions. Face changes as you were an explorer during a journey, an adventurer on his/her quest towards a treasure.

Simplify your life by eliminating as many distractions as possible and by detecting priorities, sorting them by importance.

Do not procrastinate but commit yourself to take care of your priorities. And if you feel you need help or support, look out for it, find a coach, get trained, and improve your education.

Focus on tasks and activities that have an uplifting effect on you, engage in actions and relations that can galvanize you.

You will see how quickly these essential corrections will lead you to control your fears, embrace change, and unlock your Spirit of Adventure.

Joseph R. Fraia

My Discovery

When was the last time you experienced those feelings of anxiety, frustration, or a sense of not being in control of your life? Now think about why you may have felt that way. Chances are, they stemmed from a "fear of change" - whether it was a change you knew you should make or an unexpected change that would disrupt your life in some way. Here's the thing: *change is the one constant in life*. It cannot be helped or avoided, nor can it be controlled. What we CAN control is how we react to change. Understanding you can control your reactions to change can lessen the debilitating power you give it. I was once in a toxic relationship that lasted much longer than it should have because of my "fear of change." I feared the loneliness, but I also feared letting go of the distraction it had created to not face some issues about myself. Whatever it was that broke the camel's back, I knew I was done. I didn't know what my future would be like without him, but I knew it would be better. Joseph in the previous paragraph spoke about our fundamental needs for safety, security, and stability. Had this relationship offered me safety? No. Security? No. Stability? No.

The first tool, **Discovery**, is about developing and embracing our "Spirit of Adventure" and defeating our "Fear of Change." From the unknown can arrive wonderful opportunities not possible if one remains stuck. How does that old proverbial saying go? *"You sometimes have to close one door in order to open another."* Closing the door on your "Fear of Change" will allow for other doors to open.

In our conversations, Joseph asked me when I realized I had my "Spirit of Adventure." I didn't know how to answer it, so, instead, I asked myself when *didn't* I have it? One particular example came to mind. Let's call it "The Paris Dilemma" as I will go back to it throughout the book. After I graduated college, I was lost. I found a job as a paralegal in a law firm that would pay the rent. That Fall, a friend of mine living in Paris told me to "just come." I had spent my entire Junior year of college in France, so it wasn't a foreign or scary concept. I was 22 and had no idea what I wanted, so why not go? When I told my father, he gently suggested that I try the "9 to 5" thing for a while instead. He didn't threaten me, but my own fear of his disapproval led me to allow someone else's opinion or the fear of disappointment to influence me.

Now that my daughter has graduated college, I have made a conscious decision not to intervene with her life decisions post-college based on my own personal experience. The beautiful thing about being young is the ability to try something new with very little worries. Life will still be there, waiting for you to mold it.

I have already mentioned a recent experience with my son, a sophomore in college, but fully online due to Covid19. He loved his school before the Pandemic. He loved the football games and his fraternity and everything that goes with attending a Big 10 school. Sadly, all that changed, and he struggled with the new learning format through two semesters. He shared with me his reasons why he wanted to take the Spring semester off. I told him that I fully understood but that he needed a Plan B - a job! Next thing I know, he's on a plane to

Sun Valley, Idaho, to be a ski bum, but with a job. I was very excited and happy for him. He was going out of his comfort zone and into the unknown. He found his "Spirit of Adventure"! He was secure in his decision to forgo a semester, and he was excited to experience something new and different. He had to manage his money earned and problem solve, but he also spent three months in beautiful Sun Valley and ended it with a trip to San Diego before heading home. Not bad! School would be there waiting for him.

When I agreed to co-author this book, my "Fear of Change" entailed conquering any doubts I had about my abilities. I could either do nothing or I could defeat my fear of not being a legitimate contributor. With regards to my "Spirit of Adventure", my past experiences had somehow already prepared me. And I used the tools I learned along the way to help make it as smooth of a process as possible.

Where I also recently needed to address "Fear of Change" and find my "Spirit of Adventure" was around discussions of a geographic relocation. After 20 very happy years in New York, my husband and I decided to move South. If you had asked me a year ago, I would have said there was no way I was going anywhere. My children grew up here, we made wonderful friends, I loved the access to New York City, and we genuinely loved where we lived. But something happened. Visions of what our new life could look like appeared, and I very much liked how it looked. There was some introspection involved, taking a deeper look into my subconscious and unconscious. I realized that I had held on to my life in New York for so long because I had moved at least 15 times before landing in my home of

18 years. I needed stability for myself and my children. I wanted the dust to collect and not think about packing another box.

While we would also be distancing ourselves from our families, the flight back to New York is under two hours, allowing for frequent visits for our "fixes" of family, friends and New York City. In exchange, we were starting a new chapter, an adventure, and the chance to acquire a second home somewhere dear to my heart. That introspection and opening of my mind made letting go of my life in New York easier. In fact, I am truly looking forward to the move. It's remarkable that once you have taken the "Fear of Change" out of the picture, how refreshing and exciting the new picture and its possibilities look.

Deborah Sanguineti

CHAPTER 2

Discovery, Mission.

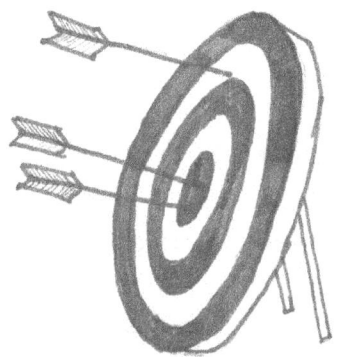

Let's now move a step forward in checking which tools we need to have in our toolbox to turn our life into a treasure hunt.

For that purpose, it is essential to be or become aware that, once you have learned not to fear, but to embrace, change, and you have ignited your "Spirit of Adventure', you have to make the conscious decision of embarking yourself in a journey, a quest, an enterprise with a task, a goal, an objective.

We need to take what at the beginning feels like a leap of faith, a jump in the void, a dive into dark waters: you need to adventure in uncharted territory. You need a **Mission**.

a. First of all, it is fundamental to realize that in life, we have two powerful engines, energies that can set us into motion: creativity and sexuality. We are beings of intellect and instinct, and now we know that Change is an inherent condition of human nature. We know that the fear of change is the cause of our demise, but, on the other hand, we also know that when we take control of that change, fear disappears, and we're ready to embark on the journey of our life.

b. You know you possess the **Mission** tool if at the moment in your life you feel passionate and creative, optimistic and open, and you are enjoying a healthy libido.

Usually, signs of the **Mission** tool are the perception of ourselves as the right person, at the right place, at the right moment. As the person who fits in his/her job, family, relationship, career, and therefore is allowed to express his/her ingenuity and resourcefulness. We feel confident, engaged with the present, and our trust in people is higher; we enjoy and succeed in our social skills, we are on the lookout for new relationships and new opportunities. We feel comfortable in our own skin and enjoy our intimacy, specifically in our sex life. That is when we enjoy satisfying sexual experience/s, joyful and playful erotic activities.

You can apply this tool in any area of your life: you experienced an inconvenience, a delay, a glitch, an issue, but you kept yourself together and stayed focused on your goal; you were waiting for the right moment to take action, and when you saw the right opportunity you seized it; you are at a crossroads in your life or need to make a turn in your career/relationship, and you assess the situation, evaluate your options and make the decision you see best suits your interests; you are experiencing erotism or sex in a satisfying or transformative way, you are comfortable in your intimacy.

You know you possess the **Mission** tool when you feel purpose driven. When you acknowledge and recognize you are doing what you are good at, and this supports your confidence in your overall abilities, to the point that, if faced with a new, unforeseen, or unprevented situation, you feel you will be able to take care of it. Your creative energy and sexual impulses are channeled and wired to defined activities and people, complementing your personality, and you are at ease expressing your genuine Self.

In such a mental and emotional environment, you are in the ideal position - in a manner of speaking a sort of 'state of grace' - to take that leap of faith or jump into the void we mentioned earlier in order not to let *Fear* hold you back or stop you.

c. You know you haven't mastered the tool in question yet if you experience a lack of, or repressed, creativity, an undecipherable restlessness, a pervasive sensation of dissatisfaction or un-accomplishment, a feeling of inadequacy and/or social numbness.

In other circumstances, you might suffer emotional isolation because you feel you do not have enough of 'what it takes' to be socially appreciated. On the opposite side of this spectrum, you might believe you are better than the people around you, hence they do not deserve your time.

On a different level, you might experience sexual dysfunction or withheld intimacy, or you might indulge in promiscuous/licentious behavior as well as in fetish fantasies.

The examples above are proofs of unevenness in our life, or a lack of balance that ultimately deprives us of the **Mission** tool.

How can we detect and recognize that asymmetry?

d. Some of the signs of this imbalance we have discussed earlier in this paragraph: you might feel held back either by lack of creativity or excessive isolation; you might be experiencing low libido, fear of intimacy, and fixation on sex. You might feel driven/dragged away by being overemotional, hedonistic, or manipulative.

In this scenario, your intellect and your instinct are not aligned, and the primary impulses of creativity and sexuality are either overcharged or drained and cause one common effect: immobility.

And immobility is the nemesis of the **Mission** tool.

How to solve the imbalances and regain stability

Realize that we have two powerful engines: creativity and sexuality. Our creativity is made of our intellect and instinct. We all have them, so we have to put them to use, knowing that intellect is the sum of what we learn, and instinct is the innate biological factor and the natural impulse to take action.

Channel your creative energy and sexual impulses.

You need to focus or stay focused on your objective, channel your impulses and energy to tackle the topic/issue at hand and use your creativity to look at the process of achieving your goals as a journey, an adventure.

Determine in what direction your instincts could lead you and decipher if they are consistent and aligned with your purpose and goal, your mission.

Detect activities you have a natural inclination for or are passionate about and focus on those.

Find a contest, a competition, a group where you can compare your skills and engage with people with the same interest.

Reflect on your intimacy and what you'd like to experience, and how.

Joseph R. Fraia

My Mission

Now that you have your **Discovery** tool, fear should no longer be such a dominant factor in facing change. The next step is defining your **Mission**. Once you have done it, the balancing of intellect and instinct comes into play. We all have intellect simply based on past experiences and what we have learned from them. How we choose to use it is a different matter. We also all have instincts. We are born with them, as they are part of our DNA, but how we choose to channel them is also a different matter. It is here where the balancing of intellect and instinct determines your **Mission's** outcome.

I knew that writing this book was a huge opportunity. I didn't know all it would entail, but I knew enough (my intellect) to take it on, and my instincts included realizing and being open to new opportunities. When it comes to working closely with someone, my instinct is to give as much as I can. But my instincts can also lead me to communication issues when I get frustrated. I've learned from past experiences (my intellect) what not to repeat (my instinct), and therefore, I have consciously chosen to guide my instincts into more positive directions. Doing so helps "keep it together" when feeling frustrated or faced with a setback.

Writing this book with Joseph was not easy because I had to take self-awareness to a whole new level. I realized things that had been laying around in my subconscious and unconscious for a very long time. For this mission, I consciously remained focused, and I channeled my impulses for the betterment of this mission. Both intellect and instinct were balanced.

Not all journeys get you the **Mission** tool. Let's revisit my "Paris Incident." I shared how lost I felt after graduating college. I took a job that paid the rent, but I never truly enjoyed it. What had attracted me to the idea of going to Paris was that a purpose or a mission was somewhere in that experience. I could feel the possibilities. My intellect told me I could do it because I had already lived in France. Part of my instincts were naturally leading me there because of how I tended to embrace adventure and I was naturally drawn to Europe. I was good at meeting people as well, and believed opportunities would present themselves once I got settled. Sadly, what was more powerful was instinctively having a lack of confidence. That instinct controlled the scenario - or should I say I let it control the scenario consciously or subconsciously - hence, creating an imbalance. I didn't have the confidence to push back on what my father was suggesting for fear of disappointing him. Eventually, after that experience, I learned to consciously channel this impulse and remain balanced as often as possible.

Having children gave me a new **Mission** - one that I loved and embraced 100%. I needed to be a good mother because consciously, I didn't want to repeat the mistakes my own mother had made with my brother and me (intellect). And fortunately, I was instinctively prone to motherhood. But at a certain point, I needed more. My next **Mission** came through my grandmother. She was an accomplished artist with an extraordinary story. We were very close, and when she passed in 2012, I began the task of carrying on her legacy. I searched out exhibition opportunities and worked on "reintroducing" her to the art world. It continues to be a balancing of intellect and instinct to this day, and it remains a **Mission** I am so grateful for to this day.

Deborah Sanguineti

CHAPTER 3

Discovery, Mission, Map.

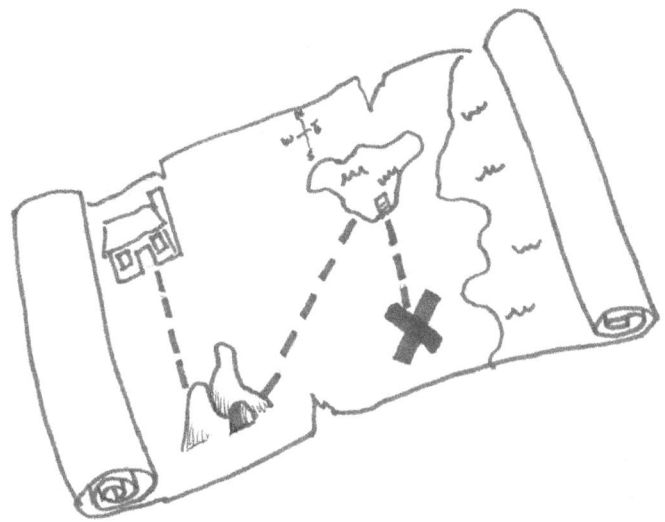

In our progression to understand which tools we need to have in our toolbox to turn our life into a treasure hunt, we can now move a step forward.

For that purpose, it is essential to be or become aware that we need a map in our quest to find our treasure. We need to get to know who we are and how we look at the world. We need to run a SWOT analysis (Strengths – Weaknesses – Opportunities – Threats) of our condition to improve how we interact with the social environment and the people around us.

The summary below can help us to memorize and internalize more easily the steps we will describe below.

<u>Internal – Individual sphere</u>

Strengths are our Liberations

Weaknesses are our Constraints

<u>External – Social sphere</u>

Opportunities are our Assets

Threats are our Vulnerabilities

Strengths maximize Opportunities – Weaknesses maximize Threats.

The importance of this tool cannot be stressed enough, especially considering its complementary relevance in connection to another tool, the Team. We will see in chapter 5 that your internal communication and external communication are preparatory to the Team tool.

The SWOT analysis involved with the **Map** tool helps you dealing with your internal communication (which is the engine of what shortly we will identify as our *individual/personal sphere*). If you do an honest review of your Self and your worldview with the **Map**, you can focus on your external communication (an essential part of the *social sphere*); hence you will be fast-tracked to get the Team tool.

a. The **Map** tells us about the importance of the realization that in life we need to ascertain our character and personality (strengths and weaknesses), as well as the context in which we operate and the social environment around us (opportunities and threats).

We are beings who live and grow up in groups. This condition defines our existence: to maximize the chances of properly and effectively perform in our groups (teams) (family, siblings, work) and communities (neighbors, church, friends, hobbies, and interests), we need to be or become aware of our *individual/personal sphere* as well as of our *social sphere*.

The individual sphere is determined by the strengths and weaknesses of our personality and character and determines the measure of the knowledge and awareness we have of our Self.

On the other hand, the social sphere consists of the opportunities and threats around us related to the groups and communities we are in, and it determines our worldview, how we look at the events that occur in our lives.

When we are capable of balancing and acknowledging our individual/personal and social spheres, we corroborate our self-esteem, strengthen our willpower and personal responsibility, and – consequently – how we get to know what we are good at, so we can increase our chances of self-realization and success.

b. You know you possess the **Map** tool if at the moment in your life you feel confident, in control, empowered, driven, and you have a good self-image of yourself.

Usually, signs of the **Map** tool are showing integrity and respect for yourself and others, feeling confident and outgoing, having a 'problem solving' attitude, being calm and reflective.

Once you detect and become aware of the **Map** tool and how to use it, you will find yourself way more comfortable in reviewing and assessing your behavior as well as in evaluating and gauging the opportunities and threats life presents to you.

In our popular imagination, sedimented after centuries of tales, stories, legends, and accounts, whoever wishes to find a treasure needs a map. In countless novels and movies, often the map is the 'MacGuffin' everybody is looking for and chasing across perilous adventures.

Somebody might argue that the map is the most important piece in a treasure hunt because it tells you where the loot is located.

And the **Map** tool in this book is no different. The **Discovery** and **Mission** tools are indeed the very prerequisites you need to acquire *before* you start the journey; they are the run-up you need in order to take the leap of faith necessary to overcome your Fear of Change and embrace your Spirit of Adventure. The process we described in the previous two chapters is an intimate and internal one that requires self-introspection and self-discipline and remains within the borders of your own mind: instinct and intellect. Once you have internalized and made yours those two steps, the third one that starts the hunt in the physical world is the **Map** because you are ready to focus on your personality and character, as well as the context and environment right around you.

You know you possess the **Map** tool when your strength and courage support you. You build and exercise your willpower rationally and thoughtfully. You experience healthy and solid self-esteem. You are also aware of your weaknesses, the traits of your personality that can set you back or hold you back, the features of your character that pull you out of your right course, mess up with your balance, and your healthy routines. In such a status, you are in the best position to take advantage of the opportunities presented to you and avoid the threats that, along the way, can prevent you from fulfilling the potential of those very same opportunities.

In the **Map** tool, awareness is the light, and ignorance is the darkness. Only in the light we can see. And we need to see, to be aware of our Strengths, Weaknesses, Opportunities, and Threats if we aim to manage them and use them to our advantage to succeed and find our Treasure.

Indulge in and use your Strengths.

Contain and confine your Weaknesses.

Assess and pursue Opportunities.

Detect and manage Threats.

That is the *mantra* the **Map** tool teaches us when we acquire it.

c. Instead, you know you haven't mastered this tool at the moment, or just yet, if you experience manipulative tendencies or misuse of power, or if you suffer from low self-esteem or control issues.

You might realize you have been experiencing being overly controlling, competitive or power-hungry, or the opposite, and you have been suffering from low self-esteem or control issues, feeling powerless, experiencing poor digestion, or chronic fatigue.

Remember that the **Map** tool requires you to run the SWOT analysis we discussed at the beginning of this chapter. Here, in particular, we need to focus on our *individual sphere* and review our behavior with honesty and fairness before moving to the next step and getting to the *social sphere*, in which opportunities and threats are assessed.

As a matter of fact, when we do not rely upon and use our strengths but allow our weaknesses to take over, we are imbalanced, and we set ourselves up to miss opportunities and let threats becoming real and harmful.

d. Clear signs of that imbalance are that you might either feel held back by low self-esteem or a sense of being powerless; you are suffering an inferiority complex or may feel driven/dragged away by perfectionism. You have been over-critical, domineering, or driven by power hunger.

On the one hand, you might have also been overly apathetic and kept procrastinating commitments or realize you are often 'taken advantage of' and feel lost and purposeless.

On the other hand, you might realize you have been judgmental, stubborn, critical, and aggressive to the point of even bullying people close to you.

It is clear at this point why the **Map** tool is so important, why it is so decisive to acquire it and master it.

The **Discovery** tool in chapter 1 teaches us to embrace change. The **Mission** tool in chapter 2, to use intellect *and* instincts/emotions to manage changes. The **Map** tool to learn who we are and how to react to changes.

How to solve the imbalances and regain stability

Be confident and alert, corroborate your self-esteem and courage to (anticipate) be ready for opportunities that might come on your way. Keep your weaknesses in check and be vigilant about the threats you may encounter during your journey.

When we miss opportunities and when threats become real, the harsh truth is that we did not use our strengths. Instead, we indulged in our weaknesses. Accountability is the most crucial step towards awareness. To hold yourself accountable, you must be aware of an issue and put yourself in a position to control and master it and progress towards betterment. That is when we connect our *individual sphere* with our *social sphere,* and that's when we thrive in life.

Indulging and succumbing to your weaknesses increases the likelihood of you suffering the realization of your *Fears*. Instead, using and relying on your strengths increases the probability of you taking advantage of the opportunities Change presents itself to you and unlocking your Spirit of Adventure.

Joseph R. Fraia

My Map

In order to obtain the next tool, the **Map**, I first needed to understand better who I was as an individual and socially. Joseph described doing so through a SWOT analysis: Strengths - Weaknesses - Opportunities - Threats. Our individual spheres focus on our personal strengths and weaknesses. Our social spheres focus on opportunities and threats "out there." I like to think that a quick SWOT analysis can be done for almost all situations you may be facing.

Take writing this book and the tools I acquired so far. I had my "Spirit of Adventure" in hand (**Discovery**), and I was more consciously aware of my intellect and instincts and how to direct them in a positive direction (**Mission**). Now, honestly and humbly, I needed to reevaluate my own strengths and weaknesses in my personal sphere. While I had some degree of self-confidence to say yes to this project, I still had self-doubts if I could be a genuine contributor. The two can go hand in hand, and often they do. In this case, my strengths (self-confidence, embracing my "Spirit of Adventure") outweighed my weaknesses (self-doubt). Another strength was being open to what Joseph would say. This led to us having very good dialogues from beginning to end, even when things, at times, weren't going as smoothly as we may have liked.

Another SWOT analysis example would be in regard to managing my grandmother's legacy. My strengths are passion for my mission and a genuine love of all aspects of art. I am comfortable talking with people about my **mission**. My weaknesses are that I lack formal education in art history and curatorial studies. My brand, "Deborah Sanguineti, Curator of Nenne Sanguineti Poggi's U.S. Collection" isn't exactly well known. So, which one will dominate here? Strengths or Weaknesses? I'm still at it, so clearly, my strengths have prevailed.

Once you understand your strengths and weaknesses, you can move to your social sphere, where you analyze your opportunities and threats. In every situation, be it family, work, etc., there are opportunities and threats all around us. The trick is to identify them and figure out what to do about them. Let's use a hypothetical example. Say I was at a cocktail party and started chatting with someone who worked at the Italian Cultural Institute. It would seem the perfect opportunity to talk about my grandmother, the *Italian* artist. Networking! If there was no place to exhibit her work, I could offer up a way to get involved with the organization and possibly meet other people drawn to Italian culture. See where this is going? This is the **Map** tool guiding me to potential opportunities. Instead of simply accepting the person's "no" to exhibition possibilities and threatening my end goal, I've extended the potential opportunity this connection may provide. I've used my strengths of being able to talk to people (my individual sphere, ME) in this particular social sphere, where I evaluated any opportunities and threats.

There are some threats you can't avoid, like someone's behavior towards you. No matter how hard you try, that person will continue to threaten your well-being. But you have the control of removing or distancing yourself from that threat. It may not be easy, even painful, but now imagine the opportunities you've allowed to happen that can make you happier. Identify those threats and figure out the best way to handle them, especially now that your "fear of change" has been recognized and addressed.

Let's go back to the "Paris Incident." My weaknesses ate up any strengths I had. The self-confidence and belief I had in myself to handle the situation and the desire to go were so strong that THAT should've been enough for my **Map**. I had already evaluated the opportunities and threats, and I was comfortable with the unknown parts. But my fear of disappointing someone was greater and held me back.

The SWOT analysis can be challenging or quick, but it works for any situation if you are honest with yourself first. By not recognizing and using your strengths and allowing your weaknesses to take over, you risk missing the opportunities and allowing potential threats to become real and potentially harmful.

Deborah Sanguineti

CHAPTER 4

Discovery, Mission, Map, Compass.

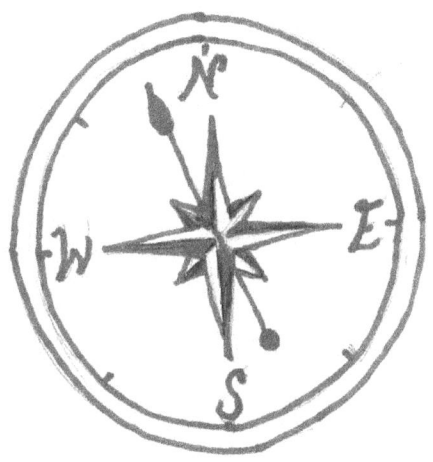

In our quest to find the Treasure so far, we have acquired very useful tools: Discovery, Mission, and Map. They all are powerful instruments that can help and support us in this adventure we call Life. They are instrumental because they represent those personal, individual, internal features we need to nurture and develop *inside* ourselves; they reside in our consciousness and are the components of what we call *Self*. We are now ready to move one step further ahead. For that purpose, it is essential to be or become aware that having limits and limitations is part of our and everybody else's life. We all are flawed beings who inevitably make mistakes along the journey of our lives. We all share one clear common denominator: many times – even despite the best intentions and efforts – assessment and decisions we make turn to be wrong. Error, mistake, fault, and miscalculation are all very familiar words because they characterize our lives and those of the people around us.

There are also circumstances and systemic factors that determine environments in which individuals and groups have to face constraints, uncertainties, and adversities beyond what a single person can control. Being aware of those circumstances humbles us down but also makes us stronger.

They humble us down because they are a constant reminder of the lesson we learned with the **Discovery** tool, which is that - in life - changes happen, and we have little control over them. Therefore, inflating our ego with the illusion that we can have or achieve total control of what happens to us is not and will never be beneficial to us. But that awareness also makes us stronger. As we learned through the **Mission** and the **Map** tools, when we focus on ourselves, train our instinct and intellect, and get to know our Self at the best of our capabilities, then we can master our attitude and how we approach and react to the inevitability of *Change*. We must avoid diminishing our ego and lessen it to the point of constantly fearing change: we can instead embrace change and ride with it, which ultimately enables us to actually increase our effectiveness in steering it in a direction more favorable to us.

What is important to acknowledge and realize now is that - what we just described - is common to the entire human race: we are all flawed beings who have to face uncertain odds, having limited time and resources, and trying to make sense of our existence. In this endeavor, I need help, as you do, and as any and each person in this world.

We all share the same experience and the same destiny: that is the heart of this fundamental truth, the very base and the common denominator that put us in the position of understanding and connecting with each other.

The awareness of that truth needs to be the **Compass** we need in our Hunt for the Treasure, the tool that points towards the direction we want to pursue, the instrument that can guide us in adverse circumstances or uncharted territories of our lives.

a. First of all, it is fundamental to realize that our relationships define us. We were born in a group, our family, and we evolve and mature surrounded by other people. The people who are around us, in part we choose, in part, they happen in our life. We have to deal with others one way or another; therefore, feelings like <u>love</u> and <u>self-love</u> and behaviors such as <u>compassion</u> and <u>trust</u> need to be raised, nurtured, developed, and refined. And those feelings and behaviors go two ways: surely, we need to learn how to deliver them to others, but it is just as important to learn how to seek them from others and to communicate our needs.

b. You know you possess the **Compass tool** if at the moment in your life you feel peaceful, loving, compassionate, tolerant, warm, and open.

Especially compassionate is the quality we want to focus on. While "empathy," "sympathy," and "compassion" are three words that many use interchangeably, they are not synonymous with one another. Let's take a closer look at how to differentiate them.

Empathy refers to feeling what another person is feeling.

Sympathy means you understand what the other person is feeling even without feeling it yourself.

Compassion means your feelings have prompted you to take action to solve the problems, fill the needs, relieve the suffering of another person. What moves you is a connection at a human level that also urges you to level a disparity, raise an opportunity or promote progress.

According to the latest implementations in integrative therapy, compassion does not stop at the ability to understand and identify with the needs of others and relate to them, but also includes the ability to take action and work to solve them.

And that's why, in our journey to find the Treasure, compassion represents the **Compass** that can guide us, give us the right direction to take, because Discovery, Mission, and especially the Map could be of poor use if we do not know which route we must set sails.

If, in our Hunt for the Treasure, we combine our Introspection with our Spirit of Adventure and prioritize detecting and solving others' needs in our journey, we would immediately see the benefits and advantages in any area of our lives: family, work, career, relationships. Because not only we would set ourselves to be in the best position to positively and constructively improve the life around us and therefore ours too, but we would also be able to mirror our experiences with other people's ones, leading to a more profound and authentic understanding of what and who we are. As we clarified earlier in this chapter, compassion goes two ways: outward, solving other's needs, and inward, asking for other's intervention when we need it.

In integrative therapy, compassion has a much broader and more inclusive meaning than the one used in everyday language. It refers to that ability embedded in humans' hearts and ingenuity to relate to other people's problems and take action to remedy them.

In that sense, compassion does not limit its sphere of action to personal or social issues but includes economic and political ones, as well as technological and professional ones.

At the very core, people who get involved in their local communities or become representatives in their districts, similarly to entrepreneurs who invent new products and services, or engineers and programmers who come up with new designs or software they all take action to find a solution moved by a force, an impulse that starts with the detection of a problem and the will of finding a solution which ultimately is meant to make everyone's life better: that force, that impulse is compassion.

Following this line of reasoning, it is easy to notice that the most successful people and companies are usually those who solve the problems that are most difficult or affect the most people.

The jeans fabric was invented to provide heavy duty workers with comfortable and resistant pants, disposable diapers were invented to increase toddlers' hygiene and health, the dishwasher was invented to alleviate the life of caregivers in the household, wireless communication was invented to increase people's mobility, fireproof materials were invented to make houses safer, and so on.

In marketing, there is the notion of 'Unique Value Proposition,' which is a statement that clearly tells your potential customers how they will benefit from your offer, how your products or services will address their needs and solve their problems, and what makes your offer different from the competition.

It is clear now why the **Compass** tool is so important. Because it is the moral and humanist beacon that can inform our thoughts and our actions, and be the ethical reference for our decisions and our actions when we think of others.

It is also the paradigm we must use in our journey to get to the Treasure when we think of ourselves, the care and love we must have for our own needs, the courage to admit to ourselves and others that we need help or support.

a. Usually, signs of the **Compass tool** are being empathetic and compassionate, showing self-esteem and selflessness, as well as forgiveness and acceptance, experiencing deep, meaningful connections, and centered awareness, understanding, and discernment. You feel bright and positive, sharing and spreading 'good vibes' around you, or you might find yourself finding peace and transcending your ego.

b. You know you possess the **Compass tool** when you easily connect with others and let others connect with you; you are at peace and embrace acceptance and inclusion. You are also able to be honest and truthful about your feelings and limits and recognize when you might need help or support and seek it: this way, in making it easier for others to understand you need their help, you are actually more effectively helping yourself.

c. On the other hand, you know you haven't mastered this tool yet if you suffer depression, lack of self-discipline, or experiencing difficulties in relationships.

In other circumstances, you might feel unloved, indulge in self-pity, neediness, clinginess, uncertainty, undermined by fear of rejection.

On a different level, you might experience an excess of entitlement, jealousy, or arrogance, finding yourself blaming others for your troubles or depending on others too much to the point that you cheapen yourself away, squandering your time and energy in pointless relationships.

d. Clear signs of this imbalance are that you might either experience shyness and loneliness, or you are experiencing trust issues, and you have been intolerant, bitter, or hateful; or you may feel driven/dragged away by lack of empathy, being jealous, codependent, self-sacrificing or 'giving too much' to others aimlessly.

How to solve the imbalances and regain stability

Accept that we as humans are flawed and that we make mistakes, and, because of the latter, we may be in some sort of need.

Understand also that there are circumstances and systemic factors that can affect the situation of an individual or a group, which can cause them to be in some sort of need as well.

Because of these truths, the **Compass tool** teaches us that *Compassion* has to be the moral beacon of our actions, the ethical standard for our decisions.

Compassion translates into understanding and identifying ourselves with the needs of others, relate to them, and take action to solve them.

It also means, though, that you have to be open and receptive and welcome somebody else's help when you are in need.

In this case, you have to listen and accept somebody else's compassion genuinely.

The balance is knowing when to give help and when to ask for it.

When we are able to express our own feeling of unhappiness and seek compassion, we can learn how to be better compassionate.

Joseph R. Fraia

My Compass

The first thing I learned when better understanding the **Compass** tool was how not to confuse compassion with empathy or sympathy. While you can feel empathy and sympathy for someone else, with compassion you act on. To be a compassionate person, you don't have to become a martyr, because giving too much can bring anger and resentment. Compassion means that when you come into contact with someone who is suffering and in need, you help that person. Again, it's about action - detecting and understanding another person's needs, followed by offering a solution. It's what connects us to those around us. The opposite of compassion for me is indifference, which means an unwillingness to act, a disconnection with others.

We are surrounded by people. Wouldn't acting out of care and compassion make for a better world? Would we not become more trusting of others, therefore feeling better because of it? Helping each other is what makes us happy, something we may not even realize. When you *intentionally* make someone unhappy with your words and/or actions, it is because, in some way, you are unhappy with yourself or are being deprived of something...maybe compassion from others? But before you can be compassionate with somebody else, or start taking action to go in their support, you need to start with yourself: a compassionate attitude begins with self-respect. Self-esteem, love, compassion, and trust are cyclical if you allow them to be. Compassion is the **Compass** that reaches that dark space within you, fills it with light, turns around, and leads you down a path towards a more balanced you.

The opportunity to be compassionate can be found everywhere, including in the professional world. At the most basic level, think of businesses that have filled a need. Grocery stores serve needs, as do gyms. Products have been created out of a need to ease suffering. My daughter represented a figure in one of her theatre classes named Lillian Moller Gilbert. She invented the step-on trash can and designed the triangle method in the kitchen, amongst other things, and all to ease and simplify a woman's domestic home life. While we use the word 'compassion' in a more technical way here, we are still taking actions to make someone's life better, leading to some form of success. Compassion allows you to relate to other people. Think about how important this is. Consider businesses and companies where bosses can show compassion towards employees, or where employees can show compassion amongst themselves.

I thought about how the **Compass** tool related to my own journeys, past and present. When did I become a compassionate person? Was I always a compassionate person? I'm sure my own life experiences had something to do with it. As a mother, being compassionate has always been a must. Once my children were born, I lived to serve them. Could that be due to the lack of compassion I received from my own mother? Could another mother claim it's due to the example set by her mother? It's interesting to try to be objective and ask yourself why or why NOT you are a compassionate person. The answers could be quite revealing. My truth is that my choice to be a compassionate mother has helped to forge special relationships with both my children, and these relationships will continue to bring me great joy for years to come.

When I can help someone, I feel good! Acting out of compassion breaks down fences, not only for the person you've helped but for you as well. It leads you down the path of becoming less concerned within yourself and more connected to others. The greater the acts of compassion, the better you become at problem-solving, which becomes incredibly useful during any part of your journey.

Let's revisit "The Paris Dilemma." Had I had enough self-love for myself, I probably wouldn't have feared some sort of rejection from my father for going to Paris. Who's to say he would have rejected me? The point is that the problem began with me. I could have shown compassion for his fear of me leaving for something a bit 'unconventional' by telling him that I needed to do this for me while I appreciated his advice. And in all fairness to him, in order for him to show compassion, I should have told him how unhappy I was. When we are able to express our own feelings of unhappiness and seek compassion, we can learn how to be compassionate better. Ultimately, the true value of the **Compass** tool resides in the fact that it teaches us when to provide compassion as well as when to ask for it for ourselves.

Deborah Sanguineti

CHAPTER 5

Discovery, Mission, Map, Compass, Team

Our hunt for the treasure is halfway through. When we know we possess the Discovery, the Mission, the Map, and the Compass, we are ready to work on our **Team** tool.

For the sake of clarity and simplicity, I want to point out that we will use the term **Team** in quite a dense and profound way, with an omni-comprehensive meaning.

As a matter of fact, according to the different circumstances and situations we might happen to be in - the different cultures and traditions, and the places and times - people use a wide range of words to describe the same concept: fellowship, tribe, crew, group, family, friends, brother in arms, squad, and the list could go on and on.

The **Team** tool is not one-dimensional, *au contraire*; it is multifaceted and applicable to the different contexts you find yourself living in, but it is of fundamental importance to acquire it to accomplish the task of your journey and find the Treasure.

To do that, we need to be or become aware that we function in groups, we need the constructive contribution and support of people who are either necessary or accessory to our purpose, and we can only do that if we can communicate and share, but also listen and relate with others.

Communication is the key to the Team tool.

What are the main elements that compose what we call communication? Answering this question allows us to maximize our chance to accurately detect the areas where we need to prioritize our efforts.

We can identify three sets of communication: inner, social, and business.

Inner Communication is what we have described and analyzed in Part I as Introspection. It is the conversation we have between our Higher Consciousness and our *Self*, the voice in our head that speaks the mind, analyzing our actions, comparing memories, and assessing the morality of our behavior and its consequences.

Social Communication is what we have earlier called interaction/relationship. It is the conversation we have with others, the exchange of opinions, thoughts, and emotions, verbal or non-verbal, that allows us to experience what is called socialization, *'the process by which individuals acquire social skills, beliefs, values, and behaviors necessary to function effectively in society or a particular group'* (American Psychological Association Dictionary of Psychology).

Business Communication is the process of sharing information between people within and outside a work environment. Effective business communication is how employees and management interact to reach organizational goals. Its purpose is to improve organizational practices and reduce errors.

***

When communication in those three areas is good, fluid, transparent, and authentic, it is efficient and effective in building and managing productive and constructive interactions, leading to good teams.

A good team is one in which members are well-coordinated, have a clear understanding of the respective roles, the structure of the group, and the goals.

When communication is bad, scattered, unclear, and dishonest, it is dispersive and dull, generating unproductive and destructive interactions, leading to bad teams or, even worse, to solitude (in which we put ourselves) or isolation (in which others put us).

A bad team is one in which members are disorganized, confused about their roles, the group's hierarchy, and the goals.

We live in the Era of Communication, yet - when it comes to our individual ability to communicate - it is astounding how little attention our society pays to the importance and ramifications of how we conduct our communication skills: for the most part, the latter is simply considered a trait of someone's personality, a feature of the character, and there is a disheartening fatalism, a blind acceptance about it. We usually say people are extrovert or introvert, more social or solitary, talkers or listeners, lone crusaders or team players, but we should go much further than simply labeling others or ourselves. We should question these attitudes, scrutiny them and not end up merely accepting them as they are.

Once again, you could realize you are living in a cage with invisible bars or find yourself constrained by people or circumstances.

If so, did you put yourself in that cage, or someone else did it? What sequence of events determined your restriction?

These are indeed fundamental questions to which there are really only two possible answers: either you put yourself in that situation, for which you need to hold yourself accountable if you really want to solve your problems and acquire the **Team** tool, or other people did. Therefore, you need to question if those persons should be in your team (spoiler alert: very likely they shouldn't).

As a matter of fact, we should regularly question how healthy our ability to communicate with our *Self* and with others is and what we can do to detect and fix any insufficiencies. We also should use and valorize our natural propensities, assess and improve our and others' skills to avoid setting ourselves up to fail the essential task of finding/building the **Team** we need to find our Treasure.

Unbalance in communicating with our Self or others

To better understand how vital the **Team** tool is and how it is affected by our communication skills, we will now briefly list some of the most common symptoms of unhealthy communication so that you can run your self-diagnosis test.

Problems within inner communication, the one with our *Self*, and that we usually call introspection and self-awareness manifest as frustration or aggravation, leading to excessive insecurity and volatility or excessive entitlement and arrogance. Mild or pronounced signs of these states are indicative of a one-rooted cause: **unbalance of internal communication**.

Problems with outer communication (social and business), the kind we entertain with others and that we usually call interaction and relationship, usually lead us to be or become solitary and leery or abusive and dominant. In the first case, our insufficiency causes us to fold into the protective shell of loneliness, a passive attitude that spares us from having to interact in a social environment. In the second case, our excess leads us to flatten any confrontation with aggressiveness, an active attitude that, in this case, gives us the illusion of control over our reality.

Mild or pronounced signs of the above states indicate a one-rooted cause: **unbalance of external communication**.

If you find yourself relating to any of the above characteristics, you do not have to be afraid to admit it to yourself. Do you remember what we learned with the **Discovery** tool? We can control fear and defeat it; Higher Consciousness gives us the key to embracing change and our Spirit of Adventure. Acknowledging that there is an imbalance is the first step in solving this issue and continuing marching on to obtain the **Team** tool.

How to Build a Team

According to the American Psychological Association Dictionary of Psychology, a team is '*an organized task-focused group. Members of such groups deliberately combine their individual inputs to pursue a common goal and are typically cohesive and united.*'

The above is the very core of the concept of team and can be applied to the more basic and essential teams (i.e., a couple or a family), as well as to the more elaborated and structured ones (i.e., a club, a company, a sports organization, a regiment of soldiers).

The words of the great philosopher Aristotle powerfully resonate to this day: "*Man is by nature a social animal; an individual who is unsocial naturally and not accidentally is either beneath our notice or more than human. Society is something that precedes the individual. Anyone who either cannot lead the common life or is so self-sufficient as not to need to, and therefore does not partake of society, is either a beast or a god².*"

After more than 2,000 years since the Greek sage wrote his masterpiece, we still are no gods and still spend our lives trying to acquire education and behaviors to emancipate ourselves from our initial state of ignorance and amorality; hence we still need to be social beings.

It is clear at this point that sociality is an inherent quality of our condition, but then the real matter is not 'if' we are or not members of a group, but more accurately 'in what kind' of group we are: a good one or a bad one?

A 'good' team is one in which the synergy of the members allows the group to achieve its goals more efficiently and effectively than each member would have done individually.

A 'bad' team is one in which the misalignment of the members causes the group to disperse energy and resources and ultimately to lose sight of the respective tasks and the common goals.

Now it is time to move a step forward and learn *how* we can turn a bad team into a good one and a good team into a better one. The skill we need is 'Team Building.'

---

[2] Aristotle, Politics

Visualize your ideal team and turn it into reality

How do we build a team? What characteristics do we - and the other members - need to possess or develop to do it?

The definition by A.P.A.'s Dictionary of Psychology of 'Team Building' can help us again to clarify this subject.

Team Building is a '*structured intervention designed to increase the extent to which a group functions as an organized, coherent whole. Such interventions often involve assessing the current level of group development, clarifying and prioritizing goals, and increasing group cohesiveness.*'

The ideal scenario in which a team flourishes is when it achieves a **shared mental model** (also called **team mental model**), which happens when *"a mental model of a work system is held in common by the members of a team. Ideally, team members should have a shared mental picture of the system and its attributes, a shared knowledge of all relevant tasks, and a shared understanding of the team's progress toward its goal. Coordination, efficiency, and accuracy will increase as team members converge on a common mental model that is accurate and complete yet flexible'*.

It does not matter if you are building a team from scratch. You need to change or evolve a team or terminate an existing team to restart a new one: the process is the same.

To achieve a shared mental model in your Team, you have to be certain and determined about your goal and the result you want to obtain with and through your Team.

You then have to visualize yourself and the other members *in* the Team and play a simulation of how the ideal team should work together.

Once this image is enhanced in your mind, you will find yourself already in the mood and mindset of taking action and turning that visualization into reality.

Therefore, the next step is to share the goals and results with your Team and make sure each member is aware of their respective roles and tasks.

Now you have to work to make your actual Team matching the one you imagined and visualized.

You must keep that image always present, make sure that the team members understand and acknowledge why they need to behave and perform the way you are asking them to do.

You have to regularly remind your Team of the goals everybody is working for.

If and when there are miscommunications and misunderstandings, they need to be addressed and solved in the name of the commitment everybody took to achieve the shared goals.

You have to incentivize your team members to honestly review each other's behaviors and their own, assess them compared to what is required to achieve the common goals and what needs to be done to assure success.

You will see how much faster and more effectively this kind of Team can achieve its goals and push progress, development, and innovation. And it is because your Team now has a **shared mental model**.

You and your Team will be able to turn issues into opportunities, problems into tasks, and, more importantly, a <u>need into an ambition</u>: that is the essence and true power of the **Team** tool.

The Team tool makes you better/more effective and makes others better/more effective.

a. First of all, it is of fundamental importance the realization that in life, if usually we are aware that other people's behavior influences or affects us, we are less aware of (or pay less attention to) how our behaviors have repercussions on other people; therefore, we like it or not, whether we are aware or unaware of it, we constantly and incessantly communicate with people around us, and our ability to function in society, and in every aspect of our life really, is enhanced by how clearly and effectively we communicate to others.

Communication is a two-way interaction. We communicate when we talk or listen, we write or read, we act or observe.

You know you possess the **Team** tool if at the moment in your life you express yourself with confidence, you are a clear communicator and have the ability - when needed - of being diplomatic (i.e., rational, posed, fair, honest, and assertive), and you keep an open-minded approach when interacting with others.

b. Usually, signs of the **Team** tool are that you can express yourself with ease and in a clear way, you are able to listen to people with attention and let them share with you their thoughts and opinions and, more importantly, you find yourself operating in functional teams, be them family, work, side jobs, passions or hobbies.

In the previous paragraph, we came to the conclusion that when we possess balanced internal and external communication, and we actively engage in team building, we are mastering the **Team** tool, and we can apply it to any area of our life.

In your family, you are open about your ideas, feelings, concerns, aspirations, and adapt your attitude and behavior towards the different family unit members, living by example and asking them to do the same.

In your job, you are aware of your position in the hierarchy and structure of the workplace and the roles of the people who work with you; you are focused on your individual and group tasks, detect the best synergies and try to contribute to solving problems positively.

In your passions and hobbies, you contribute to building a positive and meaningful culture, seeking support and knowledge from the members with more knowledge and experience, and helping and assisting those with fewer resources and experience.

The above ones are all great indicators that you possess the **Team** tool.

c. On the contrary, you know you haven't mastered this tool yet if you are experiencing an inability to express yourself, hesitant speaking, shyness, anxiety when talking to strangers or in front of a new audience.

Feedbacks you receive from other people are that you are seen as timid and dependent, unwilling or unable to stand for your opinion, reluctant to make your case or assert your reasons.

On a different angle, you might find yourself indulging too much in gossip or criticism, talking too much without letting other people speak, keep interrupting people when they talk, or generally you talk loudly. Also, you might indulge in your stubbornness.

d. Clear signs of this imbalance are that you might either feel held back by being unable to express yourself or speak out, you have been secretive or not a good listener, or if too often you ascertain you have been misunderstood or have the sensation that people 'don't get you.' Also, you might experience the frustration of not being able to express your creative side and your imagination, which can increase your resentment towards others and push your isolationism.

On the opposite side of the behavioral spectrum, you may feel driven/dragged away by being opinionated, mouthy, or you indulge in looking for and stressing out other people's faults. You use sarcasm in a mean way, you show a lack of care for how your words might affect or hurt other people.

Imbalances in communication have a disruptive effect on our abilities to be members of a team, a family, a workplace, a community.

All the references above make pretty clear and self-evident why communication is the genetic code and the very fabric of the **Team**.

How to solve the imbalances and regain stability

We need to keep in check our inner, social, and business communication skills and work on building teams that have a **shared mental model**. That can be done by following the 12 rules below:

1. Acquire and display self-awareness
2. Talk and listen to your team with attention and care
3. Assess and evaluate the positive and negative traits of each member of your team with fairness, honesty, and ethical rigor
4. Detect and manage conflict skillfully, making sure you solve it through mediating, compromising, or straightening the wrongdoings
5. Act with compassion and firmness
6. Acquire and display the ability to develop others constructively and positively
7. Engage in tasks with self-confidence
8. Acquire organizational awareness
9. Act as a keeper of the order when it is constructive, and be the catalyst for change when needed
10. Maintain a positive, constructive attitude
11. Be adaptable
12. Engage others appropriately to keep them goal-oriented

Joseph R. Fraia

My Team

The **Team** tool is about getting from "I" to "WE" and being successful. A **Team** can be a relationship, a family, a group of friends, or a work environment, to name a few. It begins with "I" and *inner communication*. It's that little voice inside of you, telling you what to do, whether you want to listen to it or not.

Let's go back to "The Paris Incident." I can now see that 22-year-old, unable to express herself to her father, in part because she was anxious about somehow disappointing him. I didn't think my reasons for going would sound good enough to *him*, and therefore I would have never been able to express myself clearly and with confidence. My inner voice was screaming to go for various reasons, but I couldn't communicate this to my **Team** (a parent-child one). In this case, I was consciously aware of not wanting to risk disruption within that **Team**. Subconsciously, it was because I had already lost a parent-child **Team** with my mother. So, for six years, I remained unhappily on a **Team** called my job until I found a new **Team** in the cultural setting I craved.

How we communicate within our settings can tell a lot about ourselves. I communicate much differently now than I did when I was 22. Obviously, it is due to the life experiences I had and things I learned about me along the way. But what about the 22-year-olds today? How can they learn to listen to that inner voice and communicate effectively? Hopefully, this book will provide some answers.

The "WE" part comes when we are interacting in a social or business setting. Communication skills are essential to have a successful **Team**! Once you have a better understanding of yourself, your own personal needs, and those you need from a **Team** - you've taken that first and essential step in identifying if it's the right **Team**. If it isn't, you know you need to find another one. My most crucial **Team** is my family, and, for the most part, we communicate effectively. We support each other, listen to each other, and show compassion for each other. My social **Teams** - the friends I surround myself with - consist of people who share like behaviors. Because of the years I've already lived (and what I learned from writing this book), I have less difficulty kicking someone off my **Team**. Who needs the negativity that comes with it, like feeling insecure or manipulated? Think about the kinds of **Teams** you have been a part of. Maybe you played sports in high school, or collaborated with a group at work, or organized events at your children's school with a group of parents. What did you receive from your teammates? Cheers? Support? Encouragement? Help? For a **Team** to be successful, it is important to embody clear and effective two-way communication. I've always enjoyed collaborating with others. The more times I did, the more confident I became when expressing thoughts and opinions. I enjoyed listening as well and learning new things. It is also important to learn how to communicate during difficult times with respect, clarity, and confidence. When a **Team** does so, they move forward more quickly.

My understanding of the **Team** tool has brought a tangible awareness of my relationships - past, present, and future. It all comes down to communication. Understanding that other people's behaviors have certain effects on us must also understand and accept that our own behaviors affect others. A multitude of good **Teams** surrounds me. I have my family, my friends, my **Team** of Joseph and I, and my day job, to name a few. I can now reflect on some bad teams I'm no longer a part of - some by choice and others not - and I'm grateful either way because of my understanding of the importance of a good **Team**.

Deborah Sanguineti

CHAPTER 6

Discovery, Mission, Map, Compass, Team, Vehicle.

We have made it this far in our Hunt, and we are only one step away from the Treasure.

We are ready for this final effort because, in our journey, we realized the importance of:

- Overcoming the *Fear of Change* and embracing our *Spirit of Adventure* (Discovery).
- Channeling impulses (creative and sexual ones) to let our instinct and intellect lead us to take action (Mission).
- Knowing who we are and how we look at the world (Map).

- Acknowledging that we are social beings and recognizing the value of compassion if we want to live a more meaningful existence (Compass).
- Realizing that we are not isolated entities, but we function in groups that we need to understand, relate, interact with and build if we want to see progress in our life (Team).

The last tool we need is a vector, a medium, a means of transportation, essentially a **Vehicle** that can carry us to the Treasure.

This **Vehicle** is our wisdom combined with our imagination. Wisdom is the quality of having experience, knowledge, and good judgment; imagination is the faculty or action of forming new ideas, or images, or concepts of external objects not present to the senses.

We need to feed, nurture, and let both of them grow and develop inside us.

The American Psychological Association's Dictionary defines **imagination** as '*the faculty that produces ideas and images in the absence of direct sensory data, often by combining fragments of previous sensory experiences into new syntheses*,' and **wisdom** as '*the ability of an individual to make sound decisions, to find the right - or at least good - answers to difficult and important life questions, and to give advice about the complex problems of everyday life and interpersonal relationships.*'

The combination of the two is the reliable tool we need for the last step towards the **Treasure**. Because with wisdom, we assess and evaluate what we know and what we do not know, and we make decisions and take actions according to our knowledge and expertise.

With imagination, using our fantasy and creativity, we fill the gap of what we do not see or do not know.

As we pointed out in the very first chapter of this book, life simply happens, constantly causing changes. These changes are facts we better not escape from or go around to because the price we would pay otherwise is exceptionally high: a life trapped in a cage with invisible bars, a troubled existence filled with frustration, disappointment, and resentment.

To master these changes, we need to use our imagination and wisdom together in a synergic manner: we must take the material occurrences in our life and look at them from two different perspectives.

Through wisdom, we look at facts using the knowledge, education, experience we already have to make evaluations, determinations, and decisions.

Through imagination, we look at the same facts using our intuition, instinct, and emotions to conceptualize, visualize and create an abstraction that we imagine seeing coming to life.

Picture a glass half-filled with water: when you look at it, you can consider the half with water your wisdom and the 'empty' half, the void, your imagination.

The water represents the knowledge of facts you can't escape from, and the best and most effective thing you can do is look at it, analyze it, understand it so that you can handle it properly. Whereas the empty part - in the absence of direct sensory data - allows your imagination to express itself: what do you imagine is in that void space? What does your imagination tell you is happening in the empty part of the glass?

Free your imagination up and think about everything that could happen in the emptiness of that glass.

Now you can expand the above example furthermore. The room where you are now is your physical reality, but what about everything else is *not* in that room. What does your imagination tell you could be in the room that you don't see?

Let's go a step further. The building where your room is located is your physical reality, but what about everything else that is *not* in that building. Now you can expand this concept from the building to the city you are in, the country you live in, the planet you inhabit: your imagination is still there, allowing you to fill up larger and larger voids: the exciting news? The larger the void, the more space you can fill with your imagination.

Being the synergic and symbiotic combination of wisdom and imagination that it is, the **Vehicle** is the ultimate tool to find the **Treasure**. Through it, we can look at reality as a whole, the tangible and the intangible. With wisdom, we see and understand the tangible. With imagination, we 'fill the gap' caused by the intangible world and become creators of reality: what we can achieve then is <u>complete clarity over the world around us</u>, the visible and the invisible one, we can disperse the clouds of doubt and confusion, navigate the vessel of our existence through the misty fog of uncertainty and insecurity and aim towards the **Treasure**.

a. With that in mind, we can now understand the importance of realizing that once we abandon our fears, embrace change, and take control of our lives, we become fully aware of ourselves, the people, and the environment around us. We also learn to acknowledge that, to thrive and strive in life, we can't be alone; therefore, we need to take care and build relationships, but we can only receive genuine support from others by being compassionate and understanding.

b. You know you possess the **Vehicle** tool if at the moment in your life you can use and express your intuition and imagination and acquire clarity of thoughts and vision through your knowledge, education, and experience.

Clear signs that you're mastering this tool are finding yourself to be, or to be seen as, intuitive, charismatic, being at ease, meditative, and reflecting on your life, when you know your purpose and people around you see you as poised and wise, confident, and accomplished. You can apply this tool to all the most critical aspects of your life: personal, social, work, artistic. To gauge and assess the level of your mastery of the **Vehicle** tool, and have a measurement you can rely on as a standard for future reference, you need to separate you from yourself and look at your life from the outside, focusing on your general mindset and how it translates on your behavior, because the latter is what the people around you base their perception of you on.

At the very beginning of this book, I made clear that the tools we discuss are undoubtedly connected to each other and, in the ideal toolbox we carry with us in our quest for the **Treasure**, we preferably have the seven of them. Still, we also stressed out that each tool has its individuality and has its independent existence and purpose. That also applies to the **Vehicle** tool, but it is undeniable that if we already master one or more of the other tools, then the **Vehicle** becomes much more effective and powerful.

An example might help to clarify this critical point.

Imagine you own a fast ship. Its velocity can't really be appreciated if the ship never leaves the docks. Similarly, the same ship can't show its speed if it sails on rough waters and if the crew is not adequately trained or coordinated, and if the Captain doesn't have authority over the crew.

Likewise, the **Vehicle** tool it's much more stable, reliable and worthwhile in your hands if you have acquired and kept the other tools.

Having stated the decisive importance of this tool, we can move a step forward and observe how it practically plays out in real life.

Wisdom and imagination define your personality features because they build your Mindset, a state of mind that influences how you think about and then enact your goal-oriented activities.

Your Mindset directly affects your Behavior, any action or function that can be objectively observed or measured in response to controlled stimuli.

Your behavior creates Perception (of you by others), '*the process or result of becoming aware of objects, relationships, and events by means of the senses, which includes such activities as recognizing, observing, and discriminating. These activities enable others to organize and interpret the stimuli received into meaningful knowledge and act in a coordinated manner*' (A.P.A. Dictionary of Psychology).

Mindset, Behavior, Perception. Once you embrace the potential of that chain reaction and understand that mastering your **Vehicle**, your wisdom, and imagination, is what allows you to take control of your mind, to set your behavior in the right direction towards your goal, and generates the positive constructive perception in people around you that you are a proactive force for good, and optimistic, confident, driven.

Then you are ready to see beyond your physical boundaries and achieve self-realization, happiness, and success.

c. You know you haven't mastered this tool yet if you experience a lack of direction, clarity, or purpose: therefore, you cannot see and focus on the 'bigger picture' of your life. **In the void of knowledge and imagination, you can be easily influenced by other people or circumstances, who will fill that void for you, but with *their* values and beliefs**. This way, though, you only get pieces of a puzzle that do not belong to your design, and that is why, if you are experiencing these difficulties, you are also confused about your goals, and you keep doubting yourself.

d. Additional clear signs of the imbalance in wisdom and imagination are that you might either feel held back by poor judgment, lack of focus, or poor imagination, and you feel trapped in your physical reality. Or you may feel driven/dragged away by delusions, obsessions, intellectual immobility, and so you often experience a lack of progress in your life, the people around you, your environment. This state may cause you to feel or be spaced out, lost, worrying, or seen as living in a fantasy world.

You inevitably experience more stress and insecurity with dimmed knowledge and imagination because your ability to assess situations, make decisions, and take actions are clouded, short-sighted, shattered.

You might experience a general feeling of discouragement, submissiveness, unfulfillment. All the above are essential indicators, and if you see them in your life, this is the moment you need to stop and have a conversation with yourself.

How to solve the imbalances and regain stability

Build your knowledge and wisdom by enriching your culture and education (read a book, listen to an audiobook, attend a seminar, watch a documentary, find a mentor or a coach, etc.), and gaining everyday life experiences (family, job, hobbies, friends, sports, etc.). Train and feed your imagination by letting your mind go on a free flow of thoughts, images, desires, and aspirations (picture a blank canvas, a photograph yet to be taken, or having wings taking you to your destination), and observing and absorbing everything around you (listen carefully, pay attention to details, lay back and watch life unfold).

Use the tools of this book to define a solid and focused mindset that you will put into practice with your behavior to determine your reality and the perception that others have of you.

Joseph R. Fraia

My Vehicle

The final tool, the **Vehicle**, is your mode of transportation, taking you to your Treasure. On your journey, you have amassed different forms of wisdom and imagination. All of this wisdom and imagination are powerful! And the more you master each tool, the more powerful your **Vehicle** becomes.

For this specific journey, writing this book, I did a recap to confirm I had acquired the tools thus far. I checked off the **Discovery** tool because I embraced my "Spirit of Adventure" - attempting something new - and I conquered my "Fear of Change" - fear of failure as well as fear of success and what that could entail.

The **Mission** tool was checked off because writing the book became my mission - my purpose - especially during Covid, when life was slower. I trusted myself and Joseph that I was going to be up to this task, and I took my leap of faith. Once I started, I wanted to see it to the end. And here I am, proud to hold this book in my hands.

The **Map** tool was checked off after doing my own SWOT analysis, where I gained wisdom by acknowledging my strengths and weaknesses. I also recognized this opportunity to be a rare one and not to pass it up despite any potential threats.

With the **Compass** tool, I learned what compassion truly means and what it can bring to your life when you become a compassionate person. I also realized the importance of being able to *ask* for compassion, and that the two were equally important. Joseph and I had our challenges while writing this book, like scheduling issues, life getting in the way and slowing the process down, and the dreaded writer's block. But never once did we not feel and act with compassion nor fear being able to ask for compassion.

We persevered together. My **Team** tool was checked off because of this. We were also surrounded by other teams that offered much needed support and encouragement. My own family even contributed to the book with the illustrations.

I gained so much wisdom and imagination by collecting these tools - wisdom and imagination I will hold on to consciously when in other situations, and the fuel needed to take me to my **Treasure**, in this case, this book.

Life can just happen, and with that comes inevitable change. I have learned to handle change with a *conscious awareness*, and with the help of the wisdom and imagination I already had, but also gained with this journey. Completing this book was *my* reality. Some of it was tangible (calling for wisdom based on experiences), and some of it was intangible (my imagination using intuition and instinct to fill in the unseen). Ultimately, it created a new *mindset* with myself, which *I* controlled. Your mindset can only be reflected through your behavior, which will then be perceived by others. Think about how *mindset, behavior, and perception* can actually work to your benefit or your detriment. I use the example of representing my grandmother, The Artist. Despite no formal degree in art history, curatorial studies, or marketing, I was determined to take this challenge on. I've had my share of disappointments, but I've also had my share of successes. My behavior, how I conducted myself, wasn't a reflection of my failures.

It was responsible for my successes - perceived by many in positive ways - someone who is passionate about her cause, willing to do the work, and is capable. I have enjoyed the rewards and opportunities due to my *mindset and behavior*, and I have no intention of slowing down despite the possible failures I might experience along the way.

Deborah Sanguineti

CHAPTER 7

Discovery, Mission, Map, Compass, Team, Vehicle, Treasure.

The Treasure

At the beginning of this book, I anticipated that we were about to undertake a challenging adventure, a burdensome task, to achieve Higher Consciousness through:
- Introspection, using our Integrative Identity Development System™, and the Enhanced Ladder of Inference to take the reins of your unconscious, subconscious and conscious mind and defeat the Fear of Change.

- And through the Spirit of Adventure, using the Seven Tools for the Treasure Hunt™ to navigate the perilous waters of our fate and find out how to live a purposeful and meaningful life.

Without Introspection and the Seven Tools, we are like a leaf in the wind, a shallop in the ocean, a drop of water in the mist: at the mercy of the elements. And that is, unfortunately, how so many people live their lives: unaware of the value and the potential of their Self and their Higher Consciousness, passively carried by their own existence, and inevitably out of reach of what we have called the **Treasure**, the ultimate reward we can achieve in our Life.

The alternative path, the solution I offered you in this book, is to get ready, to gear up, to embark on the journey of your life with a fully developed personality and carrying a box full of tools, so you are prepared to face and solve the challenges that will occur to you, and in doing that you develop the skills that will lead you to the **Treasure**.

Introspection is how you program your unconscious, subconscious and conscious mind to be the floor (foundation, ground, base) of the Enhanced Ladder of Inference that is in line and consistent with the archetypal person you have discovered in your *Self* thanks to the Integrative Identity Development System™.

The ladder of inference is the scientific breakdown of how our conscious thinking and thought processes work. In the enhanced version I proposed in this book, we take the instrument of the ladder a step further by pointing out how it generates a reflective loop and an action loop.

The reflective and the action loop are the yang and yin forces that collide, generating the big bang of the new universe that unfolds when we see the once invisible bars of our cage, and we break them.

The reflective loop molds and shapes our new unconscious and subconscious, while the action loop allows us to light up the spark that ignites the intuition of the very first tool: the Discovery. The intuition that change is inevitable, and instead of fearing it, we have to embrace it.

That spark, that intuition, is what I called the Spirit of Adventure, the force that sets us to take off towards the **Treasure**.

From there, the journey we have described can lead us to the awareness of how our mind works, and the Enhanced Ladder of Inference helps you acquire and master the use of the Seven Tools, taking you to the **Treasure**'s gate.

You are now standing at the threshold of the den and have everything you need to reach out to your reward: what do you need to do to finally get your **Treasure**?

You need one last step. You need to fully understand and embrace what the **Treasure** really is and represents.

In common language, a treasure is something precious, very valuable to us, and that we hold dear, a prize that changes our life and makes it better.

The definition of **Treasure** I offer you in this book is more profound. It is the physical and intellectual reward you receive for persisting and enduring the collection and improvement of the Seven Tools for the Treasure Hunt™.

The powerful analogy of the **Treasure** as the achievement we obtain in the quest for our self-development and self-awareness is meant to give you the measure of the magnitude of the attainment you can obtain when you focus and aim at the betterment of your Self.

You can achieve success, realization, satisfaction, accomplishment, and self-fulfillment if you train and prepare for it, if you have a system in place that can alert you when you are deviating from the right trajectory. Or it can boost you when you are on it, and if you are committed to doing what it takes to achieve your goals.

Our Treasure is the Higher Consciousness that will Break the Invisible Bars of Our Fear and lead us to Realize Our Potential

The Treasure is Higher Consciousness: the status we achieve when we combine Introspection and Spirit of Adventure, where self-awareness and wellness fuse together.

This book shows how to achieve Higher Consciousness through Integrative Therapy, a scientific and emotional journey that uses both rational intelligence and emotional intelligence, embodied in the Integrative Identity Development System™ and Seven Tools for the Treasure Hunt™.

This book also shows you that Higher Consciousness is not a superhuman quality and is attainable within our human cords when we set ourselves on the right path.

The **Treasure** is the ability to see what once were the invisible bars of the cage you were trapped in and to finally break those bars and set yourself free. The **Treasure** is the awareness of what you learn during your life journey and the realization that there is no true accomplishment without sharing the wisdom and compassion you have acquired owning all the tools earned during your journey.

The Integrative Therapy approach I propose sees Introspection as the essential foundation we need before we set sails for our Treasure Hunt.

The reward that we can obtain comes at the end of an experience that started with mastering and dominating our *Fear of Change* to embrace our *Spirit of Adventure,* and allowed us to acknowledge the value of creativity and healthy sexuality.

We also learned that, before we walk into other people's lives and the world around us, we need to know *who we are* and *how we look at the world*, and we would better be compassionate, pay attention to how we communicate with others, and who we choose to be part of the most significant groups (teams) in our life.

Last but not least, we now know that, if we do not work hard to build and feed our wisdom and imagination, we will always fall short and lack the final and most important step to achieve our goal.

In the chest we worked so hard to get and open, we found the most valuable lesson of all: the purpose of our life is to live a meaningful existence, in which we build ourselves to be resilient, driven, grounded, compassionate, creative, charismatic and wise.

Therefore, our life's purpose is to become a champion of Human Nature, live by example, and be a positive force for the betterment of yourself, the people around you, and the ones we come across with.

The **Treasure** you find at the end of your journey is also that You have ***realized your potential***.

By going through the process of acquiring the **Tools** You become truly aware that:
- your life is precious and is valuable
- you are living a life worth to be lived
- the journey is more important than the destination
- the ultimate reward is a meaningful, authentic, and rich life

a. The Treasure and its Higher Consciousness allow us to reach an ideal status where we open to what is beyond our personal preoccupations and visions, and we connect with a more universal perception of what is the real purpose and meaning of life.

b. Clear signs that you have achieved the Treasure is when you experience strong belief and creed in positive and humanistic values and principles. Faith and universal love if you are a spiritual person, or – from a more general perspective – a diffused sense of confidence in your intelligence, awareness, capability of understanding, and in your consciousness.

Also, signs that you have reached the **Treasure** are that you are at peace with yourself and in your environment; hence you experience joy, you feel enlightened, connected with 'The Whole' while remaining aware of your individuality, you reveal your wisdom and compassion through your actions, and you are firm and determined toward your goals.

It is clearer now why earlier I called the **Treasure** a sort of 'state of grace,' an ideal situation and context where we can express ourselves at our best because we have solid knowledge and understanding of who we are and what we want, and we have also learned how not to fear change but embrace it.

We have become a force for good because we have purpose and know how to give meaning to our life. We have become experts in how to solve the issues that life puts in our way.

We are also in the best position to help others. We can be proactive and, by living by example, we can inspire or guide other people, be leaders and drive the change to positively impact the lives of those around us.

What's next?

In the previous chapters, we have established the transformational benefits of looking at our life as the ultimate treasure hunt and ourselves as the protagonist of that adventure. We have pointed out the advantage we can gain when we try to be as ready and prepared as possible to take on that challenge. And now we also know that, at the end of that adventure, we can find a treasure.

The **Treasure** is the ultimate archetype of the greatest attainment we can achieve in our existence. Like everything else in life, though, it is also inherently temporary, finite, transitory.

Let's analyze which are the possible outcomes of transitions and changes that you can experience once you hold the **Treasure**.

There are four scenarios to be considered:
1. You maintain your Treasure.
2. You take off to pursue an even higher Treasure.
3. You realize the Treasure wasn't the one you thought, and now you are after a new Treasure.
4. You lose sight of the Treasure.

1. You work to keep the Treasure you have

a. It is the case when you feel and see you have found your sweet spot in your life. At the moment, you are happy with what you have, and you want to enjoy it fully. You are comfortable with who you are and what you have achieved, especially since you worked hard to gain the other six **Tools** while attaining introspection, and you find gratification in the daily practice of how you master and use them. You are also comfortable in your context, what surrounds you, both the places and the people closest to you.

b. You do not feel the urge or the push to go out on the look for a different or new Treasure. And that is totally fine. These are the times when we usually recharge our energies, enjoy the fruits of our labor, and plant the seed of a more secure and stable future. Practical examples can be that you are doing your job well and you start a side job to have extra money you can use to better your condition; you start planning to save money or invest it for a retirement plan or life insurance; you have already financial resources and decide to make investments in low-risk assets. Or maybe you are in a relationship and decide to get engaged or get married; you start a renovation project for your house, apartment or residence; you help a family member, a friend, a co-worker who is in need; you decide you do not want to work more hours because what you have is enough and you want to spend more time with the people you hold the dearest.

c. At the same time, you do not want to lose what you have achieved because you worked hard to get to this point, and you want to enjoy what you have. And that is also totally fine. These are the times when you keep your **Tools** under scrutiny, you run periodic check-ups to assure you maintain and consolidate your skills; you also pay attention to keep the focus on the priorities you have established, you avoid distractions and behaviors or habits that in the past held you back; you select your acquaintances so that you surround yourself with positive people, especially those who are more optimistic and constructive. In addition, you can also use the signs of imbalance stressed out in the following paragraph 3 as the red flags that can warn you about the choices and behaviors that could lead you to lose the **Treasure**.

Especially the **Discovery** and the **Map** tools taught us that - as human beings - we are flawed and imperfect, we have limited control of the events that may occur to us, and not always our behaviors are determined by our consciousness since the subconscious and the unconscious can play a relevant, and sometimes, prevalent role. That truth can surely be a cause of concern but also an ignitor of awakening. And that is the curse and the blessing of the human condition: the same phenomenon can be a reason for our success or demise.

2. You take off in search of a new Treasure

This is the case when you feel accomplished and grounded, confident and knowledgeable, comfortable in your skin, and satisfied with the relationships you entertain (family, love, friends, co-workers), and yet you feel a push, an impulse, an energy from within that makes you sense that you are ready and capable of reaching an even higher level of consciousness, self-awareness, and self-realization.

This scenario usually happens when we reach a point we thought was the top but find instead that we can actually go higher. Metaphorically, it is like a climber who reaches the top of a mountain and from there sees an even higher peak and gets excited about climbing it.

The new status and mindset you have reached gaining our **Treasure** allow you to expand your vision, further your ambitions, give more in your relationships, get better at the sport you practice, improve your artistic skills, grow your company, increase your sales, get in better shape, and be even more fit and healthy.

In everyday language, we usually describe these situations as those when we decide to 'step up our game.'

It may also be the case that you realize the time is ripe for collecting the fruits of your past and current plans, endeavors, relationships and move on to the next phase of your evolution and development, knowing that the Tools you have acquired are the foundation to build an even healthier, stronger and wiser version of your *Self*.

This other scenario usually happens when obtaining our **Treasure** made us realize we need, and can, boost our commitment, dedication, and focus even further towards more ambitious and rewarding goals. The new status and mindset you have reached gaining your **Treasure** allow you, for example, to go back to school to become more qualified, obtain a license or certification, aim for an executive position, going from amateur to professional competition, add new products or services to your business or your company, invest in research and development, find new better business partnerships.

In everyday language, we usually describe these situations as those when we decide to reach 'a whole new level.'

3. You realize you want to hunt a different Treasure

A different scenario could be that, in acquiring the Tools, the level of knowledge and experience you have acquired, along with the communication skills and the relationships that are now part of your reality, make you realize that the very meaning or subject of what you considered being your **Treasure** have indeed changed.

The new level of awareness you achieved leads you to rediscover the function and meaning of the Tools so that you can now find the **Treasure** that is more authentic and compelling with the re-discovered version of your *Self*.

This scenario usually happens when obtaining our **Treasure** has the impact of a revelation, an eye-opener, a wake-up call, and the clarity achieved through Introspection, Spirit of Adventure, and Higher

Consciousness allows you to see a new meaning, a new purpose that requires for you to radically steer from your past and your routines and aim in a whole new different direction.

The new status and mindset we have reached gaining our **Treasure** allow us, for example, to decide to change job or career, start a brand new company, move to another house or city, start or end a relationship, rediscover the relationship with a friend or a sibling, realize that we have an eating disorder and start a dietary regime, or an addiction (to a toxic substance or a person) and start going clean, discover or re-discover a faith or a religion, become an expert in a field or, maybe, start writing a book!

4. You can lose sight of the Treasure

The present scenario is obviously the least desirable and favorable, but it is also more likely to happen if we cannot implement one of the scenarios described above. And in any case, since we are not perfect beings, but rather imperfect ones who try to achieve an ideal of perfection, we must be prepared anyway for the likelihood that - possibly - we might lose sight of our **Treasure**. That is part of our human experience and nature: things eventually come to an end. Also, as I stressed out at the very beginning of the book, *Change* simply happens: it's up to us to fear it or embrace it.

Remember, though, it is indeed the inherent finite nature of phenomena in our life that make them more valuable and worthy of being fully appreciated as long as they last.

And that is also why it is important to know the signs that can warn you that you are on a path to losing sight of the **Treasure**.

a. Imbalanced attributes in your life that can lead you to lose sight of the **Treasure** could be that, despite the possession of the other tools, you display cynicism, disregard for what is sacred, close-mindedness and disconnection with your spiritual sphere. When instinct and intellect are not purposefully channeled towards the betterment of your Self, and when wisdom and imagination are not put in synergy with the goal of acquiring clarity and control over our worldviews, those imbalances can become severe enough to cause a sort of block and make you experience depression, learning difficulties, weak faith, anger at the divine, brain fog.

b. When the tools acquired with this book are misused, because not directed towards achieving Higher Consciousness in the pursuit of self-awareness, but to inflate the ego and indulge in excesses, then it is likely that a person would feel or be dogmatic, judgmental, experience spiritual addiction or feel ungrounded, addicted to spirituality, craving attention, needing to be popular, or run an over-erotic imagination. You might find yourself being detached from reality (daydreamer) or indulge in a feeling of superiority to others.

c. Another misuse of the tools of this book, rooted in self-doubt and indulgence in dawdling and languor, can lead to a mental and emotional state where you feel misunderstood, you can't have fun, you are unaware of or deny your spiritual connection. You might also find yourself indulging in excessive skepticism and difficulty in thinking clearly; therefore, you might feel either overpowered or cocky and entitled, pervaded by a general sense of disillusion and meaninglessness.

How to solve the imbalances and regain stability

What do you do when you lose sight of the Treasure because of imbalances or misuses?
If you are experiencing the issues and the disconnection described above in paragraph 4.a it is beneficial to revisit and re-examine the Mission and the Vehicle Tool, so you can channel your attention towards your instinct and intellect with your imagination and your wisdom.
If the threat you are facing is the inflated sense of importance described above in paragraph 4.b, it is beneficial to revisit and re-examine the Discovery and the Team tools and focus on what we described in the previous paragraph 2 of this chapter so you can take off in search of a new Treasure and use that push and power to re-channel it in achieving a higher purpose.
If the threat you are facing is the deflated sense of accomplishment described above in paragraph 4.c, it is beneficial to revisit and re-examine the Map tool and focus on what we described in the previous paragraph 3 of this chapter so you can strengthen the will to go on the hunt for a different **Treasure**. Refreshing the SWOT analysis of the Map tool will remind you that learning what you do not want is just as important as learning what you do want, that it is important to check yourself on your strengths and weaknesses because, oftentimes,

we don't give ourselves the credit we deserve. And if you do rely on your strengths and restrain your weaknesses, the threats will evaporate while opportunities will rise again.

Joseph R. Fraia

My Treasure

I did it. I collected my **Treasure** when I completed this book. It took 16 months during a Pandemic that stirred all kinds of emotions and challenges. Joseph and I completed something I am proud of and excited to share with others. Each tool led to a higher level of consciousness, and I learned a lot about myself and how to better engage with the world around me.

I embraced the notion of change and that I can choose how to react to it. I took on the **Mission** of writing this book before really understanding what I was getting myself into, but the **Map** tool helped me recognize my Strengths and Weaknesses. The **Compass** tool was an important one to be conscious of as Joseph and I worked closely together throughout the 16 months. It led to us being a really good **Team**. Ah, the **Team** tool was especially enlightening beyond just Joseph and me. It helped me let go of some bad **Teams**, and it helped me realize things I needed to do within my good **Teams**. So much wisdom and imagination were gained throughout this process.

These are unique and challenging times. My wish is for this book to offer insight into how better to navigate through them. As a woman in her 50's, I want all women of all ages to defy "ageism" that our culture has put on us for so long, and go after their **Treasure!** You'll need to put the work in, but you already knew that.

As a mother of a recent college graduate, I want to tell all the young women and men that it's ok not to have it all figured out by the time you graduate or by some arbitrary age you think you should have it figured out.

Are you living your best life? If the answer is yes, well done! Use what you have learned in this book to help others. But if you are questioning if you are living your best life, I'd like to clarify one thing: everyone's treasure is different. Many of us feel this need to accomplish something great because all this social media has made many of us feel inadequate. If your best life is being surrounded by loving family and friends and planting the best vegetable garden you can, that's a pretty cool-sounding **Treasure**. Don't let anyone make you feel "less than." Only you can do that to yourself.

I am so thankful that Joseph trusted me to help interpret something extremely important to him - and now me. Everything I have learned I use every day. This higher level of consciousness I now feel helps guide me when I am feeling *stuck*. It has given me the knowledge of understanding that I have choices no matter what the situation is.

We all have choices, and shouldn't your choice be to live the best life you can possibly live?

The answer is yes, because the Spirit of Adventure is already in you and your **Treasure** awaits you.

Deborah Sanguineti

Afterword

I'm someone who loves to hear stories. I grew up listening to my grandmother's stories about her life and the people in it. They blew any children's bedtime stories away. What I received from these stories is the determination to be part of my own story. And what this book and its tools confirmed is to trust the pauses and work through each tool.

Branding is such a buzzword today, where everyone has their own brand. But sometimes, you need to un-brand in order to rebrand yourself. How badly do you want your treasure? If you don't try, you'll never get it. It's that simple. And maybe you won't get it, and that's ok because you did get something from your journey. I've always told my children that the worst thing one could say is "shoulda, woulda, coulda." When I'm faced with a decision, I ask myself how I'll feel if I do nothing. If I'm afraid of the answer, I know what to do.

"Life is a Treasure Hunt" gave me the tools and the clarity to help answer such questions. My hope is that it will do the same for you. And as I write this closing statement, I go back to that clarity I now possess, and I look forward to many more treasure hunts.

Deborah Sanguineti

You are now an adventurer. I know that reading this book has changed you, I know that some truths are uncomfortable, and often knowledge comes with a bittersweet prize. But you were brave and courageous, and I am proud of you.

This life is not easy, we know that, and sometimes the burden of the challenges we have to face is heavy. Nevertheless, you decided to commit time and effort to pause and look into yourself, trying to understand who you are and what you can do to live a life with purpose and meaning.

The book you are holding is the most precious gift I have to offer. I am giving you the power to grab the reins of your fate, tame the storm of the adversities that will inevitably get in your way, and unfurl the sails to the opportunities you'll find in your journey. I am giving you the tools and the method to look at life for the extraordinary adventure that has the potential to be: it's up to you to make it happen.

You have in you what it takes. You are now a Treasure Hunter.

Joseph R. Fraia

REFERENCES

Carl G. Jung, Aion: Researches into the Phenomenology of the Self

Aristotle, Politics

Lao Tzu, Tao Te Ching

The American Psychological Association Dictionary of Psychology

https://dictionary.apa.org/

ABOUT THE AUTHORS

Joseph Ralph Fraia is an expert in interpersonal relationships, an Integrative Therapy divulgator and communicator, and a trained NLP (Neuro-Linguistic Programming) mentor. With over 20 years of experience as an intuitive coach and a background as a certified New York State (NYS) Mediator, Joseph has taken his knowledge of Eastern and Western methodologies to create very practical tools anybody can use to effectively achieve self-awareness, self-realization, and healthier life in mind, body, and soul. He is the creator of the Integrative Identity Development System™ and Seven Tools for the Treasure Hunt™ and the founder of the Center for Integrative Identity Development.

Deborah Sanguineti is the curator for NSP ART LLC, U.S. Collection and a B.A. graduate at Albertus Magnus College. Fluent in English, French and Italian, Deborah has an extensive multi-cultural background enriched by her numerous travels around the world. As a woman, a mother, and a wife, she has dedicated her life to self-development and self-growth. She is the co-developer of the Integrative Identity Development System™ and Seven Tools for the Treasure Hunt™ and the co-founder of the Center for Integrative Identity Development.

For information and inquiries about workshops, seminars, group and individual sessions please contact us at info@lifeisatreasurehunt.com or check out our

Website: www.lifeisatreasurehunt.com

Instagram: @lifeisatreasurehunt

Facebook: @lifeisatreasurehunt

www.ingramcontent.com/pod-product-compliance
Lightning Source LLC
Chambersburg PA
CBHW070814100426
42742CB00012B/2359